Moksha - The Immortal Bliss

OrangeBooks Publication

Smriti Nagar, Bhilai, Chhattisgarh - 490020

Website: **www.orangebooks.in**

© Copyright, 2023, Author

All rights reserved. No part of this book may be reproduced, stored in a retrieval system, or transmitted, in any form by any means, electronic, mechanical, magnetic, optical, chemical, manual, photocopying, recording or otherwise, without the prior written consent of its writer.

First Edition, 2023
ISBN: 978-93-5621-655-6

MOKSHA
The Immortal Bliss

Mystical Tales from Ancient Indian Scriptures

PRAKASH POL

OrangeBooks Publication
www.orangebooks.in

Dedicated

This book is dedicated to
All Truth Seekers

Na Me Dvesha Ragau Na Me Lobha Mohau
Mado Naiva Me Naivya Matsarya Bhavaha
Na Dharmo Na Chartho Na Kamo Na Mokshaha
Chidananda Rupah Shivoham

There is no hatred or anger in me, no greed or delusion,
I know not pride or jealousy,
I have no duty, no desire for wealth, lust, or liberation,
I am the form of pure consciousness and bliss,
I am the eternal Shiva…

- *Nirvanashatakam by Adi Shankara*

Preface

I am taking a naïve and audacious attempt to narrate these short mystical tales from ancient Indian scriptures that are so sacred that any deviation from its core essence could be equivalent to committing a sacrilege; so very first of all, paying my obeisance before to that Supreme Being, I offer my humble prayers with sincere apologies for any unintentional mistakes and errors committed on my part while retelling and editing these stories in English, on a profound subject of Moksha.

Afterall, the diamond is a diamond even when not given a shape or after crafting it in a beautiful form, it is still the same precious stone. Similarly, how this mystical knowledge about Moksha is shaped in tales is less important than the soul & pure essence of that knowledge. I strongly believe that pure essence from each tale has remained intact.

Many scholars have already translated original Sanskrit text in English from Upanishads, Puranas, Ramayana, and Mahabharata. I have taken their works as a reference and sincerely acknowledge them in the bibliography, and I have also applied my basic knowledge of Sanskrit vocabulary and grammar studied during school days. Therefore, these renewed translations can still be referred to as a fresh version as they are not taken direct verbatim from the bibliographic references. I am just a compiler, translator, and editor of that pure knowledge and divine source of primeval origin.

Metaphysics and Philosophy have been my deepest interest of reading since childhood. My school textbooks exposed me to the work of those great Marathi saints of Maharashtra in the form of poems, bhajans and abhangas (devotional poetries). It only increased my interest in the spiritualism and philosophy. I must mention two greatest truth seeker and mystics, Saint Kabir, and Sufi Saint Rumi, their work has been always a staple food satiating my philosophical hunger. Mother of all spiritual discourses ever written on this planet, are the ancient Indian scriptures of Sanatan Dharma (Hinduism) and their mystical depth can only be measured by an infinite universe, just by taking a small dip in that realm, one can feel floating on the spiritual firmament illuminated by a bright shining light of countless stars.

The human mind is an enigma, and a biggest mystical thought appears in every human mind born on this earth- "What is the real purpose of this life, why am I here?" with every birth there has to be an end & in between these two dots of start and end, we have a life which is not a straight line but a roller coaster of all emotions, senses, tastes, desires, and experiences. So, the follow-up question arises- "What happens in this life, is it a random (free will) or pre-destined (fate) and when the death fully concludes this life, what about those sub-conscious memories, indelible desires, and penchants for the things that we have never received or enjoyed in this birth?" A karmic entangled soul would answer to this follow-up question saying, "Let that line be extended from the dot which ended it because after all in the beginning that line was just a dot, Isn't it? So, let the dot have a birth to extend a new line." But a true seeker would rather have internal monologue with Self, "When and how that line would stop extending? Afterall, one day that final dot should remain a like a dot, which is its original nature and to make this happen erasing that imperfect line is possible by eliminating those memories, desires and attachments which are fueling its extension endlessly." The dot is a soul and line is a life in this allegory. The true seeker who wants to know how to reach the original state of that dot may find his answer in these fifteen mystical tales from ancient scriptures. Scriptures have proved that there are absolutely no barriers in attaining the final state of soul, does not matter what is the age, status, race, and caste. In these stories, we find kings (Yudhishthira, Bhagiratha), ascetics (Shabari, Mudgala, Sukadeva), students (Bhrigu), children (Dhruva, Nachiketa), animal (Gajendra), commoner (The fowler); all these great inquisitors, regardless of who they are; able to acquire that knowledge and ultimate state of soul. The spiritual discourses on Moksha given by the royal sages and ascetics with wisdom (Yayati, Saunaka, Krishna, Janaka & Nahusha) acts as a guiding lighthouse for the navigation of souls towards the "Immortal bliss."

As the terms immortal salvation, liberation, emancipation are manifestation of Moksha, readers will find them often used in these tales. Attaining heaven is not same as attaining Moksha, and why it is so, can be learnt this from the story of Mudgala. The greatest philosophical discourse and book which reveals the mystical elements of Moksha is, Shrimad Bhagwat Gita, in which lord Krishna tells Arjuna various yoga systems including Sankhya to attain the highest goal of soul. The eight forms of knowledge which Saunaka mentions in the story of discourse between Yudhishthira and him, is about Yoga having eight prime elements: Yama (control and restraint), Niyama (rules and observance), asana (body postures), pranayama (breath extension), pratyahara (retreat and withdrawal), dharana (concentration), dhyana (meditation) and samadhi (liberation by union of meditator and meditation). Towards the end of book, the reader will learn that almost each of tales touches either one or many elements of yogas.

Mythology has been always challenged by the group of people with mindset of "Seeing is Believing." There is nothing wrong in it, with due respect of all rivers of thoughts, I will leave it to the reader's discretion if they appreciate the essence of these mystical tales exploring purushartha of Moksha or reject it based on mythological connotations.

It is a turn for the acknowledgements now! as I took my leisure and personal time out from evenings, weekends and sometimes holidays, to work on this very first project which is dearest to my heart, so obviously my family's patience and support has to be first acknowledged. My wife Poonam for being supportive, while I took on this endeavor & my son Amogh who always curiously tracked my progress on this book. My adorable daughter Anushka who is just fourteen years old, happily volunteered and used her impressive drawing skills to do a marvelous job of illustrations. Deepest gratitude to all those great reference books that are English translation of original Sanskrit text, mentioned in the bibliography.

Finally, a big thank you to reader, because of whom this book will find a curious seeker and companion.

Prakash Pol

Pune, India. 18th Feb 2023 (Maha Shivaratri)

Contents

1. King Janaka and Sukadeva's Perfect Liberation 1
2. Secrets of Death and Nachiketa's Self Realization 9
3. Amrit: the Water of Immortality 25
4. Lord Rama and Shabari's Salvation 31
5. Yayati And Discourse to Ashtaka 36
6. Yudhishthira's Exile and Discourse By Saunaka 44
7. Nahusha's Curse and Yudhishthira 54
8. Kausika and the Virtuous Fowler 64
9. Bhagiratha and Salvation Giver Ganga 74
10. Kamagita: Krishna's Advice to Yudhishthira 88
11. Dhruva's Immortal Feat 93
12. Moksha of the Elephant Gajendra 100
13. The Mahaprasthan -Yudhishthira's Ultimate Salvation 104
14. Bhrigu's Immortal Bliss 115
15. Mudgala's Emancipation & Immortal Bliss 119
Bibliography 128

1

King Janaka and Sukadeva's Perfect Liberation

This story is from ancient Mahopanishad (Maha Upanishad) explaining what the perfect state of liberation is, which Sukadeva attained with a complete detachment and finally with Nirvikalpa Samadhi (which is a deep state of meditation) where the knower and the object to be known dissolves, and attains just the immortal bliss, pure consciousness.

A hermit of great wisdom Rishi Sukadeva went to visit his father Srikrishna Dvaipayana, his father was living a life of ascetic at the Meru Mountain. After paying due respects, Sukadeva asked his father, "O revered ascetic! how had the wordly illusion (Samsara, which is the world of endless cycle of birth and death) came to form and by what means one can get rid of? What exactly it is? by whom and when is it emerged? Please, brief all about this in depth."

Upon enquiry by Sukadeva, his father the distinguished philosopher Veda Vyasa revealed all by answering his question, however Sukadeva showed no deference to the clarity provided by his father, as he himself was aware of that knowledge since long.

Recognizing the odd reaction of Sukadeva, Maharishi Veda Vyasa said, "O Son! I am not sure of all the aspects of this topic asked by you. In case, your query in this matter is not satisfied, go to Mithila ruler king Janaka, and take this up with him. King Janaka will address it up to your satisfaction because he has a great wisdom and the intellectual prowess. O Son! you can obtain all that you want from him."

After taking farewell of his father, Sukadeva descended the Mountain Meru. Arrived in the plains, he came to Mithila-Nagari, defended, and ruled by the great king Janaka. The door guardsmen of king Janaka apprised him about the arrival of ascetic Rishi Sukadeva, at the palace gate. They said- "O king! Sage Sukadeva, the son of Maharishi Vyasa has appeared at the gate, and he wish to see you." To test his mental disposition, King Janaka intentionally delivers the message that Sukadeva should stay at the same place till further message is communicated. The king then kept quiet on this subject for the next seven days. Then after, King called in Sukadeva bestowing full honors, but he did not hold any conversations with him. After waiting for seven days, he invited Sukadeva in the inner private yards of palace but did not show him up for another seven days. At the inner palace, Sukadeva was provided with service maids, innumerable varieties of delicious food, all these luxurious amenities failed to distract Sukadeva's mind, just like a gust of wind that cannot move the mountain from its position.

In that private palace too, Sukadeva remained calm, fearless, virtuous, and exalted like a full moon.

When his character and conduct is fully tested, Rishi Sukadeva was invited for a direct conversation with the king Janaka. The king bowed with obeisance, finding him joyful, asked in a humble voice, "O respected Sukadeva! you are fully contented. Please let me know what you wish now?" Eager to know the answers to those questions, Sukadeva replied, "O eminent teacher! Kindly enlighten me on how this worldly illusion has come to form and how is it eliminated?" The great intellectual Janaka described with substance all the things which were previously briefed by his illustrious father.

Sukadeva replied, "O excellent teacher! I personally have gained ample knowledge of it and upon asking to my father, Vyasa, he also told me one and the same, you have also reiterated that same and the sacred books (or shastras) also affirms it. The illusion is formed due to the choices acquired by the mind, and it is when that choice is gone, it ceases to exist. It is true that this world is deplorable, then what is the meaning of this, all that is there? O great king of wisdom! please elaborate the realistic position. My mind is misled about the understanding of this world; please, clarify the facts, to calm my anxiety."

The king Janaka then said, "O Sukadeva! Let me tell you about this knowledge in depth. Please, hear it with full attention. This knowledge is a gist of all knowledges and enigma to all mysteries. Therefore, the one who acquires this knowledge achieves the liberation from this life immediately."

The king Janaka explained, "The mind is cleansed completely when this visible world is firmly neglected viewing it null and void altogether. Moment this sense is produced, the adherent obtains eternal peace in that moment itself. The person giving-up all desires is the best sacrifice, and this perfectly cleansed state is recognized as an emancipation by the wise. O Sukadeva! Those beings, absorbed in the absolute and pure desires, living a meaningful life and all-wise in the matters of wisdom, are called liberated from mortal entanglement. The attachment to material possessions is a bondage and diminution of desires is known as the salvation."

King Janaka continued, "Desiring penances, one who leaves the habitual longing of material pleasures is only known as a liberated being. One who is never afflicted by challenges, neither gets happy nor sad, is a liberated being. One who enjoys freedom from human weaknesses like pleasure, suffering, fear, lust, anger, and pain etc., is a liberated being. One who can easily dispose-off the ego driven desires and adheres to the goal of sacrifice is truly a liberated being.

One who is not attached to any materialistic desires and strives to stay introversive (that is, not devoted to outward senses), who like in a deep sleep is without passion is known to be living a liberated life. The man who takes delight in contemplation of the supreme spirit, whose mind is complete and pure, who does not expect anything from the mortal world by the virtue of his amiable and modesty nature is known as living a liberated life. One who lives in the world without any affinity is known to be living a liberated life. Whose heart is free from attachment to sensuality and full of wisdom is living a liberated life. Busy in his own work, the man living beyond anger and envy, pleasure, and pain, good and evil, yearning for fruit or ambition is known to be living a liberated life. A man performing his deeds by sacrificing the ego, pride, envy, despondency, aspirations is living a liberated life.

Such person likes the liberated life without physical world attachments, he keeps himself devoted to work without aspiring for gains or fruits. Who has completely renounced the physical view or observance (of world) is a liberated being. One who treated different tastes equally like bitter, sour, salty, pungent and accepts whatever food is offered is a liberated being. Who lives in a total contentment be it old age, death, distress, or prosperity is a liberated being. A person who has forsaken all the emotions resulting from good and evil, joy and misery, birth and death from his mind is truly a liberated being. Who is free from worries and joy, with pure mind having equal outlook towards the elation or depression. Who has relinquished from the mind, all desires, all aspirations and plans, all firm intentions, is a liberated being. Person whose mind is unwavering and determined all the stages like birth, sustenance and death is truly having conduct of a liberated being. One who does not envy others and rarely hope anything from others, calmly faces all the good and bad incidents that needs to be faced on account of past deeds (present life destiny) is truly a liberated being. One whose aspects about worldly pleasures are completely restrained, uses his mind but do not follow stimulations from mind. Although he is part of material wealth of the world, but he remains passionless like a religious devout treating that as other's wealth, such a fully liberated being senses the presence supreme soul within his soul.

When his life is over, he leaves the state of liberated being and achieves the state of liberation without body like a stationary wind. Such a soul, neither moves nor rests, such soul surpasses real and unreal, neither near nor distant to anybody. Bodyless state is profound and astounding. In this state, neither there is a light nor there is darkness seen. A component of truth which is undefinable and inexpressible remains in that state. That is neither null nor having form, neither visible nor vision, does not contain any mass of matter. This remarkable element's nature is simply unimaginable. He is entire in entirety, neither truth nor false and not even their mixed form, he is beyond soul and existence both, He is conscious but at the same time it is without mind and boundaries. Ageless and most auspicious, it is flawless with no beginning, middle or end. He is considered to be in the form of vision in the middle of observer, observing and what is observed. O Sukadeva, there is certainly nothing which can surpass this.

You appreciate yourselves this philosophy, and you have known from your father that one is bonded to one's own aspiration and get emancipated by having a desire to overcome that aspiration. You have achieved that detachment from all pleasure giving and visible materialistic objects. All that is to be acquired, is acquired by you with a completely sensitive mind. You have attained Brahman (supreme soul) and state of liberation being. O Sukadeva! You can see external & most external and also internal and most internal, but still does not see both (that is, remain uninfluenced as onlooker). You are being witness to this in a perfect state of liberation."

After gaining the philosophical insights from King Janaka, Sukadeva achieved peace, as his suffering, fear, the tension, queries, and desires all were diffused. Then he moved to the peak of Meru Mountain for the perfect meditation (Samadhi). Like a flame lighted without oil for many thousand years, Sukadeva achieved the inner conquest by making him thus, with meditation (Nirvikalpa). Merged with the ocean, water droplet takes the same form; Sukadeva too merged his liberated soul, making it free from blemishes of desires, passions and thus attaining purest mind, sinless and all divine.

2

Secrets of Death and Nachiketa's Self Realization

This tale is a complete Kathopanishad (Katha-Upanishad), which is a primitive source of knowledge about the death, liberation, and moksha explained by ruler of death himself. This katha (tale) goes like this-

- (Part 1) -

At the Visvajit sacrifice, to gain heavenly rewards, Vajrasrava gave all his material possession as a religious gifts and donations. He was having a son; his name was Nachiketa. After seeing all the sacrificial donations made by his father's worldly possessions, a thought entered into Nachiketa and asked his father repeatedly three times: 'Father, to whom will you give away me?'- due to this repeated query of Nachiketa, his father said in irritation, 'To Death, I sacrifice you!' To keep the words of his father, Nachiketa decides to face the death, he says to father, 'See those who have lived before and see those who are living now, like a seed of a grain the mortal being degenerates and like seed of a grain, again emerges.' He convinced his father to sacrifice him to death. Nachiketa reaches to the Yamaloka, the kingdom of Lord of Death. Yamaraj was not present in his abode that time, however when he returned after three days and he understood that Nachiketa has not received the hospitality that should be conferred to a learned Brahman; Yama says- from last three nights you have stayed in my abode without eating, in your reverence I return you three boons. Nachiketa said, 'As a first boon, when I return to my home, my father may love me as before.' Lord Yama immediately granted him this boon saying, 'You father will leave his anger when he finds you coming back from the trap of death.'

On second wish, Nachiketa said, 'O Yamaraja! you have a knowledge of the Agnividya (learning of fire). Please, let me know this Agnividya which is known to the people for attainment of heaven. Those who reside in the heavenly regions relish exemption from death. This one, I pray you as my second boon. I am curious enough to know and please, explain that learning as the second boon, as you already have given the privilege to ask for.'

By telling Nachiketas that fire dwells hidden inside the heart of all creatures, he explained it further to Nachiketa; revealing secrets about how fire is from the beginning of the world, including what and how many bricks and process of building to make sacrificial fire. Nachiketa repeated this acquired knowledge before Yama. Then Yama said to Nachiketa, 'a one more boon I confer you here today'- This fire would be recognised in the world by your name. A person who has kindled this triple Nachiketa-fire, leave behind in advance the clutches of death, with miseries overpowered, delighted in the heavenly regions.

This Nachiketas is your heavenly fire, which you have chosen as second boon. For the third boon, Nachiketas; choose!

Nachiketa said - This doubt that when man is deceased, some says, 'He is alive,' while some says,' 'He is not (dead),' say others. I am eager to know the reality behind this, and this is what I want as my third boon. Yama said, O Nachiketa! Even the gods do not have clarity about this. It is correct that it cannot be easily realized. O Nachiketas, choose! Another boon. Nachiketa said, 'O Yama, no other boon is alike to this one.' Yama tried to persuade Nachiketa, he asked, choose hundreds of sons and grandsons, innumerable cows, mighty elephants, precious metals, and horses. Choose entire earth as your abode. And yourself live as much as you wish. This, if you think an equal boon, choose-wealth, and long life! A noble man on earth, O Nachiketas, be you. I will grant all your desires that you wish to enjoy.

Whichever desires are difficult to acquire in the physical world, for all of it you can make request.

These heavenly maidens (beautiful apsaras) with chariots, such indeed, cannot be easily obtained by men. But O Nachiketas, enquire me not on the topic of death.

Nachiketa said, these are all ephemeral things and have a definite end. O Lord of Death, even the shining energy of all the illuminating powers, will diminish one day. Reveal me on this state of demise of living beings! I would not prefer any other boon, than this mystical realm.

Moksha - The Immortal Bliss

12

-(Part 2)-

Yamaraja said Nachiketa - The Shreyas *(Superior)* is one and the Preyas *(Pleasurer)* is another. Both these having different objectives, tie up a person. Out of these two, one who chooses the Preyas, he deviates from his goal, while for Shreyas, the goal is within reach. Both these Shreyas and the Preyas come to a man.

By looking at both, the wise man discriminates. The man of wisdom selects the Shreyas over the Preyas. The ignorant and stupid man chooses the Preyas. You have let go all the pleasant desires of material world.

Ignorance and Wisdom are completely opposite. Nachiketa, you have a great desire of gaining knowledge! Physical and material world desires do not attract you. The men who are in deep darkness of ignorance, self-centered, thinking themselves knowledgeable, in this whole world, are in a delusional state, just like a blind person shown the way by another blind man. The state after death is not understood by these men who are immature, heedless, and deluded by wealth and material desires. These men thinks 'This is the world! And no other world exists!', Such men over and over, falls under my reign.

"HE" who is hard to reach by many even by hearing and not easily understood even after hearing. Amazing is such a teacher, one who is proficient. Amazing will be such knower when it is proficiently taught! and if HE is to be well understood it should not be proclaimed by an inferior teacher.

Unless it is not taught expert teacher, one cannot go that place. Because HE is incredibly more profound than what is of profound. This Atman or Self is not attained by mere logical reasoning, but when taught by a wise teacher, it is indeed easy to understand.

And this what you have attained, Nachiketas! Ah, you are truly resolute and unwavering in truth! May we always find an inquisitor like of you.

I know that what is material world treasure is something transitory. For truly, the one that is eternal is impossible to be attained by things which are non-eternal. Therefore, the Nachiketas-fire has been created by me, with things which are perishable and yet I have obtained the one which is constant, eternal, and immutable.

O Nachiketas, you have experienced what is physical world and material desires and pleasure, yet you are being wise rejected Preyas (Pleasurer) with a strong resolute.

That HIM who is hard to be perceived is entered into the hidden, cavern of the heart, and who is primeval and resides in the depths of inner Self-being. By means of Yoga and meditation this Self knows HIM, such wise man leaves joy and sorrow behind.

A mortal will rejoice, after having heard and fully comprehended this, and understood the subtle Self. This is because a mortal has attained the knowledge which is true source of happiness. Hence, this dwelling of truth is open to Nachiketas.

Nachiketas said: That which is neither virtue (dharma) nor vice (adharma), and which is neither past nor future, and which is beyond all of these, please explain me that.

Yama said: The supreme word which all the Vedas venerate, and which is all proclaimed in austerities; desisting it men live the life of continence and discipline *(practicing Brahmacharya)*.

That word, I will briefly explain you. It is Om! This word truly, indeed, is Brahman! That word is really the supreme! One who has knowledge of this word, earns whatever is desired by him.

This word is the best aid. That is the highest aid. He who has the knowledge of this aid, achieves a bliss in the world of supreme soul.

The Self-Soul had no birth, nor it dies. It is neither having source not giving source to anything. This primordial one is unborn, constant, eternal, unperishable. Soul is not killed even when the physical body is killed.

If the slayer thinks that he has slay or if the one who is slain thinks that he is slain, neither of them have no knowledge. The Self is most delicate than delicate and most superior to the superior, it resides in the core of the heart in all living beings. A man is free of desire and grief, his controlled senses and calm mind witness the splendor of this Self (Atman).

The Self when sitting travels far and when lying it can go everywhere, who is more capable to know than I, this God (Self-Soul) who is both cheerful and cheerless.

A wise man will never sorrow or grieve because he knows this Self, bodiless who is sitting in the perishable body.

This Self cannot be obtained by learning of scriptures nor the intellectual prowess and not by hearing it. Only by him whom the self chooses, it is attained. To that person, Soul (Atman) divulge its real nature.

The one that is not refrained from the corrupt conduct, and senses are not in control and who is not of tranquil nature and mind is not peaceful, such person can no way attain the Self even by acquiring the knowledge.

So, who could then know at where is this potent Self? The perishable beings are his food and death itself is a condiment.

-(Part 3)-

Yama continued- There are these two (higher-self and lower-self) who after their good deeds enjoys the fruit, by entering the secret cave of this heart. Men of wisdom call them light (higher self) and shadow (lower self), it is also called so by householders who perform five sacrificial fires, and those performing three Nachiketas-fire.

Thus, may we become capable to master this Nachiketas fire-sacrifice, since it acts as a bridge for them who perform sacrifice, and may we also gain the wisdom of the "One" who is supreme imperishable truth for the men of wisdom (that is Brahman), who has a desire to cross-over to other side of the shore which has no space for the fear.

O' Nachiketa! Know that this Self (*atman*) is an owner of the chariot, physical body is the chariot. Learn that the intellect *(mati-buddhi)* is the chariot-driver, and the mind (*chitta-manas*) is the brakes *(reins)*. The senses *(indriyas)* are called as the horses and the sense objects are the roads. When this Self is in harmony with the body, mind, and senses, then wise men call him 'the experiencer' *(bhoktr)*.

The person who has no power of acumen and his mind is unrestrained, and the senses are not trained like callous horses of a driver, can never reach the goal, and comes back into Samsara (mundane world of birth and death). The person who possesses the right acumen and mind fully controlled and purified, he attains that supreme goal & end of journey, reaches the supreme abode of God, and never takes the birth again.

Greater than the senses are the objects of senses and superior to the sense objects is the person's mind. Greater that the mind is intellect and greater that the intellect is Self (Atman). Greater than the supreme Self (Atman) is the unmanifested (Avyakta) and beyond the unmanifested is the "Purusha" (Cosmic Soul), beyond the Purusha nothing exists, and it is the supreme and final goal (this is a "Moksha").

This Self (Atman) is hidden in all creatures and beings, it does not shine forth; but is seen by the skillful sages with a sharp, perceptive, and fine intellect.

A man of wisdom should restrain his speech by mind, control the mind using intellect and control the intellect with a great Self (Atman) and a great Self by the supreme Self (Paramatman).

Arise! Awake! Nachiketas, and gain the understanding as you have reached the great ones. This enlightenment path is extremely challenging, razor-sharp, and unnavigable.

The one who is silent (soundless), contact-free (touchless), amorphous (formless), imperishable, also unflavored (tasteless), odorless, and immortal, who has neither an inception nor an end, greater than unmanifested by realizing this knowledge that the man break free from the mouth of death.

-(Part 4)-

Yama continued- The ignorant person uses the senses for outward purpose; therefore, man always looks outward, and not inner Self (Atman). The wise man seeking immortality, turn his eyes away from the external and seeks Soul (Atman) within Self.

The one by which, one is aware of the shape, flavour, aroma, sound, touch, and sensuous pleasures and by that one also knows whatever is not known. This truly you have to know. The one by which mortal being comprehends both in the states of dream and in the waking, by knowing such a supreme and all-pervading Self (Atman or Soul), the wise man never sorrows.

He who has a knowledge of this Self (Atman), who is a honeyeater, by being both the onlooker and relisher of objects and as a commander of the past and future, never fears anymore- This truly is That.

He who sees and recognizes him resided in the five primordial elements (earth, fire, water, air, and ether) and born from austerity (tapas), born before waters, and who having taken an ingress into the hidden place of the heart, continue in it- This is truly That.

He who knows Aditi, who leaps with Prana and present in all Devas (Aditi is a mother of Devas or Deities), who having arrived in the heart resides there and has taken a birth from the elements- This truly is That.

Just as the fire lie concealed in two-sticks and like fetus is well-protected in the womb of mother, that fire must be revered each day by attentive seekers and also by sacrificers- This truly is That.

For where the sun ascends and where it descends at setting, Devas (Gods) establish this, nobody can cross that. This is truly That.

What here in this apparent world, which is there (in the unapparent) world, person who differentiate here two, gets death after death (reborn again).

With the help of mind indeed, this is to be understood, there is no difference at all (between obvious and non-obvious), person who differentiate here gets death after death (reborn again).

The Purusha is of the size of a thumb, remains in the center of one's Self (Atman), he is the lord of the past and the future, he who has knowledge about him does not have any fear anymore. This truly is That.

That Purusha, who is of size of a thumb, is like a light without smoke, he is the lord of past and future and he is same as today and tomorrow. This truly is That.

Just like when the rainwater dropping on the top of mountain, runs above the rocks from all the sides, similarly he that notices the difference (in what is apparent and not apparent), sprints towards them in various directions.

O Nachiketas, as the pure water mixed with pure water becomes the very same pure, so becomes the Self of seer who is pure and knowledgeable.

-(Part 5)-

Lord Yama Continued- The city of unborn (body of human being) has eleven gates, thinking of HIM (Self or Atman), man should not grieve any more, and when freed, he indeed attains liberation. This truly is That.

He is the sun illuminated in heaven, He is the gas in the atmosphere, He is fire flaming in the altar; He is a visitor staying in the house. He dwells in a man. He dwells in those superior to man. He dwells in sky. He is born in water, born in earth, is born in sacrifice, and born on mountains. He is the supreme Truth and Great!

He sends the in-breath (prana) upwards and throws the out-breath (apana) downward. Seated in the center (of heart), the adorable Self is worshipped by all senses.

When this Self (Atman), who is positioned in the body is released what is remainder then? This truly is That.

No mortal whatsoever lives by the in-breath (prana) or by out-breath (apana), but the mortals live by a distinct on which these two depends.

O Gautama (Nachiketas), I will declare this to you the hidden immortal Brahman and what goes on to the self after it reaches death. Some souls go in for wombs to be embodiment into being while others go into immovable states, according to their deed (karman) and as per their knowledge.

That who stays awake when all goes to sleep, that who is pure, none goes past beyond That. All worlds (lokas) rests on him. That is That Brahman (Knowledge).

As the fire, although one, after entering the world, take different forms as per to what it burns, so acts the Self (Atman) within all beings. Though one, the Soul take different forms in accordance with what it enters in and still, it also dwells outside.

As the air, although one, after entering the world, take different forms as per to what it enters, so acts the Self (Atman) within all beings. Though one, the Soul take different forms as per what it enters and still, it also exists outside.

As the Sun, who is eye of this entire world, does not get tainted by external adulteration observed by the eyes, similarly inner Self (Atman) of all creatures is not adulterated by the vices from the world, being outside of it.

One ruler is for the Self (Atman) of all living beings who can take his one form into many other forms; the wise man who perceives him seated in oneself, will get eternal bliss and no others.

He who is perpetual among the changing, consciousness among conscious, who although one fulfills the desires of mass; the wise men who perceives him occupied within oneself, to them the eternal peace belongs.

The wise perceives that indefinable highest bliss, recognizing, This is That. How shall I understand 'This'? Does it shine (of its own light) or shine (by reflection)?

The sun shines there not, neither the moon and nor the stars; nor do this lightening shine there, very less is this fire. When he shines, everything shines, with his light all world is illuminated.

-(Part 6)-

Lord Yama continued- The primordial Aswattha tree bears its root upwards and the branches downwards. That is indeed pure. That is Brahman, the Immortal. All the world is resting in that, and none goes beyond that. This truly is That!

All that is in this universe is evolved from Life (Prana) and moves in Life (Prana). That is a great dread, like a lifted bolt of lightning. Immortal will be those who understand That.

By fear of Him the Fire flames, By of fear of Him the Sun gives illumination and heat. By of fear of Him; Indra, Vayu, and Death (Yama) the fifth, gallops along.

If a person is unable to realize him before the dissolution, that is before the death of the body, then he becomes personified again in the world of creation.

Like in a mirror, He is seen within himself (Atman); like in a dream, so in the region of departed souls; and like in water, so in the Gandharvas (angels realm); like in light and shadow, so in the realm of Brahma (abode of knowledge).

A wise does not sorrow anymore, recognizing that senses are different (from Self-atman), and their arising and setting are independent from the Self (Atman).

Uppermost than the senses (Indriyas) are the mind (Manas), over the mind is true intellect (Sattva), Further above the intellect is the mighty Self (Atman), and higher than the Self is unmanifested (Avyakta).

Higher than the unmanifested is the omnipresent and indiscernible being (Purusha). Knowledge of him the mortal being is liberated and attains Moksha.

His form can not to be seen. No one whomsoever sees him with the eye. He is conspicuous by the heart, by the intellectual powers and by the wisdom of mind. They who have this knowledge become immortal.

When the five senses of perception dissolves, along with the mind (Manas) and intellect (Buddhi), this is recognised as a highest state.

The firm controlling of the senses is called as 'Yoga.' Then one should become vigilant as Yoga arrives and leaves.

He cannot be obtained by speech, mind or by sight. How can that be obtained by him who says, "He is"?

He can indeed be attained by the knowledge of "He is" (Asti) and by real essence of both (he is both apparent and unapparent). He who recognize Him as "He is," his true nature is manifested.

When all urges residing in ones' heart are liberated, then the mortal being becomes immortal and realize Brahman (supreme knowledge)

Once all the attachments (ties) of the heart are cut part, then the mortal being becomes immortal. Such is a teaching.

There exists a hundred and one channels of the heart. One of that passes up to the center of head. Going upward by it, one obtains immortality. The other remaining ones leads to different worlds.

The Purusha, who is the measure of the inner Soul (Antaratman), is of the size of a thumb, is eternally positioned in the heart of all living creatures. With dedication man should extract Him out of his body as one draws the stem shaft from a blade of grass. One should realize Him as a pure and perpetual.

Thus Nachiketas, having gained this knowledge proclaimed by the Ruler of Death, and with the entire rule of Yoga, becomes clear from impurities and liberated from death (rebirths), realized Brahman (the Supreme Soul). And as well any other who realize the essence of the Self (Atman).

3

Amrit: The Water of Immortality

When this book is about tales of Moksha, the Amrit, a water of immortality must find its mention. The story about "Amrit Manthan," that is churning of ocean to extract 'Amrit,' which provided Immortality to Gods, is one of the most popular stories of ancient Hindu mythology too. In Ramayana, this story is propounded by Rishi Vishwamitra to Shri Rama in Balakand section and it is also found mention in Mahabharata Astika Parva of the Adi Parva, told by Sauti to Saunaka. In ancient Vedas (Rigveda, Yajurveda, Samaveda, Atharvaveda) the term 'Amrit' has a treatment equivalent to god or divine soul who has gained an immortality, that is, the one who is free from death. This is how the story from Ramayana begins:

On the request of great sage Vishwamitra, Dasharatha reluctantly allowed Rama and Laxman to go to his hermitage based on the advice of Rishi Vasishta. Royal sage Vishwamitra needed the services of Shri Ramachandra to destroy the menacing rakshasas Maricha and Suvahu, who were destroying the sacred rites and defiling the holy altar with blood and flesh.

On their way to Vishwamitra's hermitage, Lord Rama slain Yakshini Taraka and also when Maricha and Suvahu obstructed the sacrificial rites, Rama eliminated them.

After this, Vishwamitra starts out with two princes to attend King Janaka's sacrifice, during their journey Vishwamitra begins to recite the extraordinary tale of the churning of the ocean, which has also led into the fight between the Devas and the Daityas, in ancient times.

Vishwamitra said- O Rama, Diti had extraordinarily powerful sons, Daityas and those of Aditi's sons, Devas possessed great prowess, virtues and pious. Both Devas and Daityas started reflecting, 'How can we get exempted from old age, disease, death and become immortal?'

When they contemplated, it occurs to them, 'Through churning the ocean of milk (Kshir Sagara), we should acquire the divine water of immortality-the Amrit.'

After they decided upon the great ocean churning, all those devas and daityas with infinite energy made the powerful snake king Vasuki as the cord, and the Mandara Mountain, as a churn, started to churn that deep ocean.

And after churning for thousand years, the Snake Vasuki working as the churning cord, began to spew poisonous venom and bit the rocks & stones, with his fangs. And with that powerful poison emerged like a fire, this poisonous fire started consuming the whole universe with gods, asuras and men.

All gods looking to take refuge, came before the mighty god, Shiva, or Pashupati, or Rudra, urging him, 'Save us.' 'Save us.'

Attracted by the cries of the deities, Shri Mahadeva and Shri Hari came before them, Hari bearing the conch and the divine chakra. And smilingly Shri Vishnu addressed trident-bearing Shri Mahadeva, 'O Lord, ruler of the celestials, since you are the supreme of the gods, the one that has first come out of the churning by celestials, accept it. O lord, receive this poison as the first oblation.' Having spoken this, Lord Vishnu vanished. Witnessing the great distress of all celestial beings, and listening to those words of Shri Vishnu, Lord Shiva drank that terrible poison as if it is a nectar and then taking adieu of the deities, the most reverent Hara returned to back to his abode Kailash.

And then, O prince of Raghu, the devas and daityas again started the churning, that supreme mountain serving as the churning staff, began to lose its balance. Thereon the gods and the gandharvas extolling the Lord Vishnu, said, 'You are the lord of all beings, of the devas especially. O powerful, provide us your protection and support the unbalanced mountain.'

Taking cognizance of these plea, Shri Hari, acquired the form of a tortoise, approaching the sea, supported the Mandara mountain on his posterior and that Supreme being, Hari grasping of the top of the peak by his hand, began churning the deep ocean, stationed in the midst of devas and asuras.

After over a thousand years had passed, sprang a male being, the teacher of Ayurveda, a highly virtuous soul, famous by name Dhanwantari, holding in his hands a staff and a Kamandalu.

Also emerged from the skim of the churned-up waters, the splendid nymphs the glowing Apsaras. 'Ap' means water and 'yara' means to emerge from; due to this those beautiful dames were called Apsaras. O Raghava, they numbered six hundred million, and their female attendants were countless. Neither the devas nor the danavas had accepted them, and due to their nonacceptance, they stayed without lords.

Then after, O prince, the reverent daughter of Varuna named Varuni was born, looking for assent. O Rama, Diti's sons, did not admit the child of Varuna, and Sons of Aditi, accepted Varuni. Those who had did not admit her, that is, Diti's sons bear the name of 'Asuras' and those who accepted her, Aditi's sons called as 'Suras.'

And the gods became extremely happy, on having accepted Varuni.

And, O Raghava, next arose celestial horse Uchchaihshravas, who is supreme amongst horses and also jewel Kaustubha and then comes next the excellent ambrosia-Amrit, the water of immortality.

And, O Rama, there was a tremendous fight for the possession of nectar of immortality, Amrit; suras and asuras had a terrible war. And the daityas aligned together with the asuras; mighty battle was fought, terrorizing all three worlds. And when a great havoc happened and many lost lives, the all-powerful Vishnu, assumed a captivating form of Mohini, tricked the powerful danavas and seized the Amrita from their hands.

All the gods drank the Water of Immortality with extreme joy, getting served from Vishnu.

The next particular part of the story find its mention in Mahabharata- While the gods were consuming it, a Danava named Rahu started taking his share by standing amongst them, in the disguise of a god. Just when Amrita had only reached Rahu's throat, Surya (Sun) and Soma (Moon) recognized this danava and revealed the reality to gods. Having learnt that truth, Lord Vishnu quitting his enchanting female form of Mohini immediately cut off his head with powerful Sudarshan chakra. And then the massive head of that Danava, who drank Amrita in camouflage, pruned by the chakra of Vishnu appearing like a mountain peak, tossed up in the firmament and began to roar the dreadful cries. And his headless trunk, crashing on the earth and rolling thereon, caused the whole Earth tremble. Immortal head of that danava is Rahu and the immortal trunk is known as Ketu. And since then, it gives a persistent quarrel between Rahu-Ketu and Surya-Soma. And till this day it swallows Surya and Soma (that is, during solar and lunar eclipses respectively).

Finally, Lord Narayana leaving his Mohini form and together with devas hurled many terrible weapons at the danavas and asuras, which made them tremble. In this fight, the gods executed innumerable daityas.

Indra, after defeating the asuras in that great fight for the Amrit, became the king of the devas and with the blessings and help of the rishis and sages, ruled happily. Gods were immortal from that day having consumed water of immortality, Amrit.

4

Lord Rama and Shabari's Salvation

This tale is from Aranya Kanda of Ramayana and is about an ascetic Shabari who met Shri Rama during his forest exile. By the greatness of her virtuous merits accrued from the lifelong austerities, selfless services rendered to her preceptors and pure devotion to Lord Rama, cleared her path to salvation. The story goes like this.

Having learnt from the mutilated and dying bird, Jatayu about the abduction of his beloved wife and daughter of the Janaka, the King of Mithila, Shri Rama was stirred by the grief and began to weep. After performing the last honors of the divine bird, both princes combed the region in search of Sita, during the search they confronted an asura named Kabandha whose form was frightening and horrible. Shri Rama took him down and then carried out funeral rites, with that his soul soared to heaven. While entering another world, Kabandha talked to Lord Rama of Shabari, a female ascetic, and prayed him to visit her.

Both the princes, following the directions of Kabandha, progressed towards the west direction leading to Lake Pampa.

Making their way and also hopeful of meeting Sugriva, they witnessed lush green trees blossomed with scented flowers and delicious fruits, tasting of ambrosia, stretched on the mountain sides. After having overnight stay on the plains, Rama and Laxmana arrived at the western shore of the Pampa teeming with lotuses, looked at Shabari's charming shelter.

Entering that blissful haven, shadowed around by numerous trees, they saw ascetic Shabari, who after noticing them, stood up and with obeisance respectfully touched their feets. After welcoming Rama and Lakshmana, as per custom, provided water to clean themselves and wash their feet.

After some time, Lord Rama in a conversation with the female hermit, devoted to the spiritual pursuit, asked her, "Have you been able to surpass all the hurdles to attain asceticism? O you of soothing voice, does your austere practices grow daily? have you conquered your anger and tamed your requirement for food? O hermit one, have you followed your ascetic pledges and achieved an inner peace? Does serving your preceptor (Guru) produced fruit?" having thus probed by Rama, the righteous Shabari, praised by the Gods, greatly aged, bowed in deep reverence and said, "Sanctified by your arrival, I have accomplished fulfillment and my asceticism is finally rewarded. Today is a day my birth bearing a fruit and my services to Gurus are finally deserved esteem. Today my virtuous practices have found realization. O supreme amongst men, excellent of the gods, I shall achieve the celestial abode by worshipping you. O compassionate one, O destroyer of enemies, O you who does bestow grace on men, sanctified by your merciful concern, I shall achieve the immortal worlds, by your blessings, O vanquisher of your enemies.

When you had arrived on the Mount Chittrakuta, those yogis I served, mounting on the divine chariots of exceptional magnificence, left for the heaven and those virtuous and great rishis, said to me, 'Rama will stop at your holy hermitage, and you will welcome him and Lakshmana with customary hospitality. On having a glimpse of him, you will attain the ultimate realm from where none comes back.' O greatest of men, that is how those divine ascetics conveyed me, and in your hospitality, I have fetched the wild fruits and berries of various kinds that blossoms on the banks of Lake Pampa."

Listening to these words of Shabari, Lord Rama addressed her, "From Danu, I was brought to light about the glory of your Gurus and now I would gladly see it with mine own eyes, if you deem it appropriate."

Hearing these words from Rama, Shabari, showing those brothers the expansive forest, said, "O scion of Raghu, look at this forest appearing like a dark fog, inundated with wild creatures and birds, known as the Matanga Forest. In this forest my Gurus of angelic soul sacrificed to fire, their beings hallowed by mantras, also purified, and sanctified the forest as a holy place. In this forest too, there is a shrine front facing the west, where with wearied shaky hands, my revered Gurus presented flowers to their deities. O best of the Raghus, witness this shrine of matchless

grace, which, on account of energy earned from their penances, still radiates the brilliant glow lighting up all the four directions. Witness also the seven ponds, brought here on the strength of their contemplation, as, due to fasting and ageing, they were incapacitated to walk. These cloaks of bark are still wet, that were kept hanging on the tree branches after the end of their bathe and these sky-blue colored lotus flowers offered to gods during their worship have not waned.

Now you have witnessed this forest and have listened to all that which you wished to know; I will renounce my mortal body so that I be able to advance to those angelic soul ascetics which I used be in the service of, to which this monastery identifies with and of which attendant I am."

Audience to these sacred words, Rama, who was followed by Lakshmana, with a great happiness and bliss, exclaimed, "Glorious it is!" Addressing Shabari of austerity personified, Lord Rama said, "O sacred one, I have been deeply venerated by you; now depart where you want to and be happy."

Thus, taking the sanction from Rama to set off, Shabari, with matted locks, in bark clothes and a black antelope hide, offered herself into glowing fire, consequently surging through the air like a shining intense flame.

Graced with celestial jewels, wearing garlands, spreading a divine redolence, applied with sandal paste and dressed up in celestial garments, Shabari emerged blissful and illuminated the celestial heavens like a thunderbolt. By the merits of her austerity and meditations, she soared to those immortal realms where her radiant-souled spiritual gurus dwelt.

5

Yayati and Discourse to Ashtaka

This tale is from Sambhava Parva of Mahabharata, recounting very interesting journey of Yatati from the hedonistic king to an ascetic soul, and from an ascetic soul to a royal sage in the heaven and finally the fall from heaven to re-gain it back. Story is an excerpt from the main conversation that took place between Yayati and Ashtaka on the topic of Salvation. The tale of Yayati goes like this.

King Nahusha, son of monarch Ayu, fathered six sons, all noble and virtuous, named Yati, Yayati, Sanyati, Ayati, and Dhruva. Yati adopted the path of asceticism and became a Muni like Sannyasin himself. Yayati became an emperor with great bravery and merit. He governed the whole earth, carried out innumerable yagyas (sacrificial rites), revered and worshipped the Pitris (ancestors), and always praised the gods. During his rule, he brought the complete world under his control and no enemy could defeat him. The sons of Yayati were all skilled archers and embodied with good virtues. His sons were born from two wives, Devayani and

Sharmishtha. Devayani mothered Turvasu and Yadu, and Sharmishtha gave birth to Drahyu, Anu, and Puru.

Yayati righteously reigned the entire earth for a very long time. After getting to know the secret affair of Yayati with Sharmishtha, Devayani escalated it to her father Shukracharya, guru of Daityas and Asuras. In the fit of rage, Shukracharya, his father-in-law cursed Yayati that he will grow old and lose all his personal beauty. However, looking at the plight of Sharmishtha and her desire, Shukracharya told Yayati that if he is able to convince one of his sons to switch his age with him, he could be then able to avoid the curse and regain his lost youth. So, attacked by hideous decay which started eating up his physical beauty, Yayati the monarch called his sons and spoke to them, 'Oh my dear sons, I want to obtain my youth again and satisfy my desires in the proximity of young women. Please help me on this matter.' After hearing this, his eldest son from Devayani then said, 'What do you need, O king? Do you like to get back your youth?' Yayati then told him, 'Take my old age, O son! With your youthfulness, I will be able to satisfy my desires. During the time of a great sacrifice, the Shukracharya cursed me. By taking over my old age, you can rule over my kingdom. I would take pleasure with a renewed body. Therefore, oh my sons, take my old age.' No son was in position to accept to take over his old age. But then his youngest son Puru told him, 'O king, take delight once again with a rehabilitated body and regain the youth! I shall swap my youth with your old age and based on your orders, will rule your kingdom.' Pleased with his son Puru's acceptance, Yayati by the power of his asceticism swapped his debilitated old age with that of virtuous son. Yayati regained his young age with Puru's youth; with the father's old age Puru ruled his kingdom.

Many thousand years expired but Yayati, lived as potent and mighty as a tiger. And he derived all worldly pleasures and enjoyments for a great period of time accompanied by two wives. He even relished the intimacy of Apsara Viswachi in the divine gardens of the king of Gandharvas, Chitraratha. Even then, Yayati found his desires and appetites unsatisfied. One day the truths contained in the Puranas come to his mind, 'Verily, one's hunger are never satisfied by enjoyment. rather, like a sacrificial butter offered into the fire, this hunger flares up with indulgence. Even after enjoyment of all worldly pleasures on the earth with its prosperity, money, women, precious metals and diamonds, cattle, one will never be satisfied. The man that does not perpetrate any sin towards any living being, be in thinking, action, or speaking, then he could achieve to the pureness as that of Brahman (Supreme Soul). When one does not fear anything and not afraid by anyone, when one does not wish for whatsoever, when one injures no one, then he could achieve to the pureness as that of Brahman.'

The great king Yayati realized this truth that human being's desires can never be satisfied, finally he set his mind at rest, and followed the path of austerities and meditation. Yayati also again swapped his age with his son; took back his old age, and giving back his son the youth, though his own desires were unsatisfied. Appointing Puru on the royal throne, he addressed his virtuous son, 'You are my deserving and true heir and so, by you my lineage will be extended. The whole world will know my race by your name.'

Having coronated Puru as a monarch & ruler of the world, Yayati departed to the mount of Bhrigu to follow the path of asceticism. After long years of austerities and ascetic practices, he acquired splendid merits. When the ultimate time reached, he sacrificed his mortal body by the observance of fast and rose to celestial abode with his wives.

Such was a great merit Yayati acquired that he was able to travel to any place in higher celestial worlds of heaven and region of Brahma. One day Yayati and Indra happen to meet together and held conversation. Indra spoke to Yayati, 'After completing all your duties and responsibilities, you had retired into the forest, O king, I would ask you whom do you consider as equal in ascetic austerities.' Yayati answered, 'O Indra, I cannot see anyone as my equivalent among men, the gods, the gandharvas, and the rishis.' Indra replied, 'O royal sage, as you have disregarded and therefore shown disrespect to all such people that are your seniors, your equals, and also juniors, without knowing their real merits, your own merits and virtues have depleted, and you must descend now from heaven.' Yayati then replied, 'O Indra, if, at all I need to descend due to depletion of my merits, I be allowed to fall amidst those virtuous and the righteous.' Indra replied, 'O king, may you have your descent among those who are virtuous and sage, and you would attain fame. And after going through this experience, O Yayati, at no time belittle those who are your peers or seniors.'

Thus, the King Yayati, the heir of Nahusha and the father of King Puru fast descended from heaven after his virtues (noble deeds) have been depleted. And as he was plummeting, this witnessed by the royal sages including Ashtaka. Ashtaka asked Yayati who is he, and how he came descending from heavens, subsequently the profound spiritual conversation followed between Yayati and Ashtaka and other royal sages.

Some of these spiritual discourses between them which has revealed the mystical aspects of salvation goes like this:

Ashtaka asked, "O Father, How, could one obtain those superior regions where there is no come back to worldly life? Is this though asceticism or through knowledge? How could also one progressively achieve those appropriate regions?"

Yayati answered, "The men of wisdom have proclaimed that it is through the seven gates an admittance in heavenly region may be achieved. These are asceticism, charity, serenity of mind, self-control, humility, simplicity, and kind compassion to all beings. This wisdom also mentions that a man waste all these meritorious qualities due to vanity. The man considering him as a learned after acquiring knowledge, uses the same learning to destroy the honor of other people, by no means obtains those realms of immortal joy. That knowledge also does not help that learner to attain the Brahma. Learning, vow of silence, worshipful rites before fire and sacrifice, they dispel all fear. But when these are exercised with vanity, instead of getting rid of it, they give rise to fear. The wise man should neither rejoice nor grieve at insults. Because only a wise can give respect to the wise; the vicious never behaves like a virtuous being. Vanity causing statements like- I have donated that much, I have carried out lot of sacrifices, I have learned and studied so vastly, I have observed so and so vows; all these are the root of fear. For this reason, you must not entertain in such feelings. Those men of wisdom who consider its strength, the eternal and incredible Brahma (Supreme Soul) alone which always shower the blessings on men who are virtuous like you, they enjoy the perfect peace here and hereafter."

Then Ashtaka asked Yayati what is considered as Muni. Yayati then explained the characteristics and attributes of Muni to Ashtaka, "A Muni removing himself from the worldly material objects lives in the woods. Also, a learned person pulled back from the material pleasures, might become inhabitant of a hamlet living as a hermit. He would never display the vanity of pedigree, family, or knowledge. Putting on the barely enough clothes, he could still see himself as dressed in the rich apparel. Surviving on just enough food, he is always satisfied. Such a man, even though residing in a populated place, still lives in the woods. The person who has complete restraint over desires and passions, strictly observes the vow of silence, desisting himself from worldly action, accomplishes paramount goal of human life. Indeed, why should one not, worship such a man that sustains on satvik (pure) food, who does not cause injury to any creatures, who is having virtuous and pure heart, who emerges magnificent in the ascetic qualities, who is liberated from the bondage of desires, who abstains from causing injury even if approved by religion? Having become skinny by severe austerities and shrink in flesh, marrow, and blood, such a person not only conquers this world but also the celestial world. And sitting in a yoga meditation, Muni becoming dispassionate about human desires and emotions, like joy, misery, status, and insult, he then departs this world and attains eternal bliss and unity with Brahma. When the Muni takes the food without arranging for it and without any enjoyments or emotions (like an innocent infant nourishing on the mother's lap), then like the omnipresent spirit he attains one identity with the entire universe and reaches the salvation."

Ashtaka questioned Yayati, "O King, who between those two, both of whom are perseverant like the Sun and the Moon, first attains to unity with Brahma (Supreme Soul), the ascetic person or the wise man with Knowledge?"

Yayati replied saying, "The wise man by means of Vedas and of Knowledge, realizing the apparent universe to be illusion, immediately perceives the Supreme Soul as the only existent absolute soul. Those who dedicates selves to yoga meditation needs sufficient time to gain the equal knowledge, as they go by this practice alone. Thus, the salvation is first attained by wise. If a person following yoga meditation could not get sufficient time to achieve success, being deceived and allured by material world, then in his next birth life he gets advantage on account of the advancement formerly attained, while dedicated himself again to the same quest. But the man of wisdom who always perceives the eternal bliss and unity, is even though soaked into worldly pleasures, never afflicted by them at heart. Hence, there is nothing to hinder his salvation. A man who cannot attain this wisdom & knowledge, should devote himself to worship dependent on action, like sacrifices etc. But he that conducts such action, moved by the lust of salvation, can no way obtain success. His worship and sacrificial offerings do not get any outcome and join of the nature of cruelty. Piety that is performed with actions, not arising out of the desire of fruit, is for such men the "Yoga" itself.'

These queries on salvation and also various other spiritual queries were put to Yayati by Ashtaka and other royal sages, who were the descendants of Yayati. Upon getting the enlightened knowledge from Yayati, Ashtaka said, 'If there are those worlds of heaven for me to relish, on account of fruits accrued due to my virtuous merits, O king, I offer them all to you. Hence, even if you are falling, you will not fall. O, accept them, regardless of where they are, in heaven or in the skies. Let your misery end.'

Then each of the other royal sages also expressed their sincere wish to give Yayati energy of their own acquired merits. Accepting their request, Yayati attained the liberation by the virtue of the pledge of his descendants and rose back to the celestial regions, departing from earth, and earning great fame in three worlds with his deeds.

6

Yudhishthira's Exile and Discourse by Saunaka

This story is from Aranyaka Parva of Mahabharata. It recounts an incident when Yudhishthira just before the start of the forest exile is enlightened by an accomplished yogi named Saunaka, so as to lessen his mental agony of not being able to feed Brahmanas that were following him. The great secrets of Sankhya yoga are revealed by Saunaka while explaining the path to a liberation of soul. The story follows like this-

After facing the defeat at "Dyutkrida" (gambling with dice), five Pandavas and queen Draupadi set to leave Hastinapura for the forest exile towards northern direction from gate of the city. When citizens learnt about the misery faced by Pandavas in the game of dice, they became swamped with grief, and started criticizing Bhishma, Drona, Vidura, and Gautama. Citizens immersed in talking to each other, 'Oh, we are all doomed, as these immoral supported by sinful aspires the kingdom! And alas, how are we going to reside in happiness! Duryodhana holds ill will towards all elders and superiors, is devoid of moral conduct, and argues with own kith and kin. Greedy and arrogant, he is brutal by nature. The whole earth is done when Duryodhana is a monarch. Therefore, let us join with the compassionate and principled sons of Pandu with senses under control and vanquisher of enemies, and possessed of humility and reputation, and followers of virtuous practices, let us go!'

Citizens appealed to Pandavas, 'Bless you all! Where are you going, forsaking us in misery? We will pursue you, whichever place you go! we are extremely sad after getting to know that persistent enemies have falsely overpowered you! It suits you not to abandon us that are your affectionate citizens and faithful friends are always wishing your well-being and engaged in doing what is pleasing to you! As fabric, water, the earth, and sesame seeds are scented in the company of flowers, so does the qualities get influenced by the association. Truly, company with fools creates a deception that entraps the mind, whereas daily association with the wise and the intelligent leads to the path of righteous. Hence, those that desire emancipation from cycle of birth and death should have company with wise and matured, and truthful and pure in actions and carrying ascetic virtues. The association with those who possess the wisdom (of Vedas), whose acts are virtuous, and are all pure, the company of them is rather far greater than learning the holy scriptures. All those qualities exist in you, individually and together! For this reason, for our own benefit, we wish to stay amidst you who hold these distinctions!'

Yudhishthira said, 'We brothers are truly blessed since all you citizens including the Brahmanas at the forefront, stirred by fondness and empathy gives us the credit of those merits which we do not possess. However, we would like to ask you people to do this thing. You must not act, out of compassion and pity for us, in fact act in the contrary! Our grandfather Bhishma and mother, my uncles the king Dhritarashtra and Vidura, and many of my sympathizers, are there back in the capital town of Hastinapura. Hence, if you have interest in seeking our welfare, you look after to them with care, by standing unitedly with them as they are engulfed with pain and misery. Saddened by our departure, you all have come far! Return back, and let your souls be guided by kindness towards my relatives that I keep you as pledges! This is my heartfelt wish and by acting on it, you shall give me great contentment and extend me your best courtesies!'

Thus, urged by Yudhishthira the righteous, all denizens wailed loudly and with sorrowful hearts, they reluctantly moved back taking the farewell of the Pandavas.

After citizens left, the Pandavas reached to the spot of banian tree known as Pramana on the banks of the river Ganges. At the place below banian tree when it was about the sunset time, the Pandavas purified themselves with the sacred Ganges water, and spent the night under that tree. Suffering from pain and sorrow they spent that night just by taking water alone. Group of Brahmanas out of devotion trailed the Pandavas up to that location and passed the night in their company.

As the night was over and sunrise broke, those Brahmanas who sustains on the alms collected after ascetic mendicancy, appeared before the Pandavas of noble deeds, who were getting ready to venture into the forest. The king Yudhishthira again urged them to return back. Yudhishthira told Brahmanas that Draupadi and his brothers, are afflicted with sorrows and suffering on account of the losing of their kingdom & separation of relatives. They are saddened, and he will find it difficult to make the arrangements for their food.

Brahmanas did not relent and told Yudhishthira that they will look after their own food but will follow the righteous Pandu brothers in forest. Filled with regret that he cannot provide food to those Brahmanas, the sobbing king sighed with sadness and sat down.

Then a scholar Brahmana named Saunaka, proficient in self-realization, meditation, and expert in the Sankhya system of yoga, noticing the king's suffering, discoursed Yudhishthira, saying, "Every day, mortals are suffered by plenty of causes of misery and worry, but it drowns the ignorant men but not the wise men. For sure the rational men like you should never let suffering be inflicting your senses, by acting in contradiction to true knowledge, as it is filled with vice and ruins the salvation. O king, you have that insight bestowed with the eight qualities that is capable to destroying the vice and which is obtained only by learning the Shruti (Vedas) and holy scriptures! And such men like you are never dismayed, due to poverty or an affliction impacting their friends, either due to mental or physical turmoil! Listen to these shlokas that I shall recite, those were chanted in ancient times by the eminent Janaka relating to the matter of self-controlling! As this world is troubled with both physical and mental sufferings, listen now to the methods of alleviating them as I mention them here.

Illness (disease), exposure to painful things, struggle, and craving for the objects desired- those are the four causes of bodily suffering. Physical Illness can be cured by the medicines, while mental ailments are tackled with a pursuit of getting rid of them with yoga meditation. Just like water quenches fire, so does true knowledge pacify mental disturbances. When the mind comes to peace, the body finds the peace as well. It has been observed that attachment which is at the root of all mental suffering. It is this very attachment that makes every being sorrowful and invites all kinds of distress. Truly attachment is the root of all distress, fear, happiness, and sadness of different types of pain. From attachment comes all motives and out of attachment, springs the fondness of material pleasure! Both are the origin of evil, yet the first (our motives) is much inferior to the second. Just like a minor fire into hollow of tree ruin the tree to its roots, similarly attachment even if so little, consumes both morality and merit. One who has only removed himself from world's material possessions, cannot be considered as renunciation; he even though, still remains in very contact with the world in respect to its defects, can be said as really renounced the world. Liberated from every wicked passion, soul which is not dependent on anything has truly renounced the material world. That is why one should not pursue putting his attachment with either friends or the riches he has acquired. And thus, the attachment to one's own self be doused by knowledge. Just like the leaf of lotus is never soaked by water, those men competent in differentiating between the transitory and the immortal, continuously dedicated to the quest of the eternal, versed with the scriptures, and refined by knowledge and wisdom, can no way be influenced by attachment. He who gets moved by attachment is tormented by want and from this want of things arises the greed for material possessions in the heart. Truly, this want of things is sinful and known as source of all worries. The dreadful want of things full of sin leads to unrighteous acts.

Men who renounce this want of things can find happiness, but wicked can never renounce it, this want of things does not wither with the decay of physical body, it is truly a lethal ailment! It has no start and no end. Residing in the heart, it consumes the being like a fire of bodiless origin. Just like how faggot surviving on wood is swallowed by the fire that is nourished by itself, similarly person of corrupt soul is swallowed by the greed born in his heart.

Like every creature born has a fear of death, so wealthy men are in continuous anxiety of the ruler and the stealer, of fire and water, and even their kith and kin. A chunk of meat when is in air, may be gobbled up by birds; when on the ground eaten up by carnivore animals; and when in the water swallowed by the fishes; similarly, man of wealth is prone to insecurity wherever he goes. Too much wealth they amass is a curse and the one who perceives happiness in wealth, gets tied to it, they never realize true happiness. Therefore, attainment of riches and wealth is viewed as the one which enhances the greed and insanity.

Wealth is the origin of stinginess and bragging, arrogance, terror, and fear! These are the woes which that the wise men see in riches! Men go through never-ending miseries in obtaining and holding of wealth. Its consumption also is filled with affliction. And sometimes, life itself is lost by cause of wealth! Leaving behind the wealth (after death) gives rise to misery, and those which are fostered by one's riches become enemies for the acquisition of that wealth! So, when holding of wealth is full of such misery, one should not get bothered by its loss. Ignorant are always remain unfulfilled, but the wise are always bestowed by fulfillment. The hunger for wealth, by no means can be satiated. Fulfillment is the paramount happiness therefore, the wise consider fulfillment as the topmost goal of pursuit. Aware of the uncertainty of youth, physical beauty, of life, stockpile of riches, affluence and the companionship of loved ones, wise people never desire them. Therefore, one should desist from amassing of wealth, knowing the suffering attached to it. Nothing that is rich, is exempt from suffering, and hence the virtuous praise those which have relinquished the desire of riches. So, O Yudhishthira, it befits you not to desire anything! And if you would have virtue, liberate yourself from the want of worldly possessions!"

Yudhishthira replied, "O Brahmana, my wish of wealth is not aimed at enjoying it, when acquired. For the subsistence of these Brahmanas only, that I want it and not due to my greedy drive! If one cannot care and support the ones which follow him, then why one would intend to conduct a household life, O Brahmana? All living beings follow the practice of dividing the food amongst those who are dependents on them. Providing food to guest is equal to a sacrifice, and greeting with happy look, showering the attention, speaking with sweet words, showing the respect, and treating with meal and drink, are the five offerings (dakshinas) in that sacrifice. One who gives a food to weary traveler without expecting anything in return obtains significant merit, and one who is leading domestic life, pursue such habit, earns religious merit that is claimed to be exceptional. O Brahmana, what is your perspective on this?"

Saunaka said, "Unfortunately, this society is full of paradox! that which puts stigma on the good, appease the evil! Alas, driven by ignorance, emotions and their senses bonded as slave, even fools commit acts that forces them to please their desires life after life. Even with open eyes, they get adrift by indulging their senses; just like charioteer that has lost control over his senses like agitated and evil horses. When either of any six senses (seeing, hearing, smell, touch, flavor, and mind) finds its specific object, then desire sprouts forth to enjoy that object. And when this desire is indulged then it breeds the intent. This seed of intent pulls person into fire of enjoyment with a temptation like an insect pulled into flame. Blinded by sensual temptation, soaked in dark confusion and stupidity, he mistakes it as a state of joy due to ignorance! And like a wheel rolling perpetually, all creatures from desires, acts and ignorance plunges into the different states in this world, roams from one birth to other and go through entire birth cycles created by a Brahma, taking births on the tip of a blade of grass, in water, on the land, and in the air! This then is course of such beings that are ignorant, without knowledge."

"O king, listen now to the progression of the wise, that are bent on righteous virtues, and are aiming at liberation of soul! The Vedas encourage act but forsake (desire in) action. Therefore, please have these eight acts adopted by you, disowning the pride, execution of sacrificial rites, learning (of Vedas), almsgiving or donations, penance, truth (in both speaking and acting), forgiveness, controlling the senses, and relinquishment of desire --these are proclaimed as eight (cardinal) duties establishing the righteous way of life. Out of these, the first four open the way for the region of the pitris. These acts should be adopted without pride or conceit. The last four are strictly observed by the saints (pious), to obtain the abode of gods. And the pure souls should forever follow these eight paths. Aiming for salvation, those who intends to overcome the world, should always act by completely extinguishing motives, resulting into conquering their senses, strictly observing certain pledges, faithfully assisting their preceptors (gurus), controlling the diet, eagerly studying the Vedas (knowledge giving scriptures), forsaking action as a path and self-controlling their feelings (heart). By renouncing aspiration and antipathy, the gods have achieved prosperity. On account of the power and achievement of yoga that celestial beings (the Adityas, the twin Ashwins, the Rudras, the Sadhyas and the Vasus) rule all the living beings. Hence, O son of Kunti, like them, you too, by fully dissuading self from action with purpose, seek to achieve spiritual prosperity in yoga and by self-restraining austerities."

Having thus discoursed by Saunaka, the son of Kunti, Yudhishthira, talked to his priest Dhaumya and in the company of his brothers asked, 'These Brahmanas well-versed in Vedas are behind me and I am now entering into the forest. Suffered with many problems, I am not in position to support them. I am neither able to relinquish them, nor do I have the ability to provide them food: Guide me, O pure one, what should be done by me in this kind of an impasse.'

After thinking for a while trying to determine the appropriate solution by his yoga powers, Dhaumya advised Yudhishthira to worship and invoke the god 'Sun' who in the olden days supported the life on earth by generating a rainwater cycle when all the beings created were suffered from dire hunger. This blessing of sun even today supports us by producing food with agriculture on rain waters.

Following Dhaumya's advice and taking his guidance the prayers were offered to the Lord Sun. Pleased with Yudhishthira's pure devotion and hymns, Vivaswan (Sun) appeared before him and said, 'You will obtain what you are wishing for, I will give you the food during twelve years (of exile). O king, take this copper-vessel that I offer you. So long as, Queen Panchali (Draupadi) holds this vessel, without taking share of its contents the four kinds of food will never be depleted- fruits, roots, meat, and vegetables. On the fourteenth year from now, you will get back your kingdom.' After saying that, the god disappeared. From that day onwards till his twelve years of forest exile was over, Yudhishthira began to provide food to the Brahmanas which were following him, as per their wishes.

7

Nahusha's Curse and Yudhishthira

In Mahabharata, Aranyaka parva, there is a story concerning dialogue between Yudhishthira and a great Serpent in the cursed form of King Nahusha, as they came face to face in the mountains of Himalayas while Pandavas were in exile.

In ancient times, King of gods Indra, out of deep regret of killing a three headed son of Twashtri, the celestial artisan, disappeared and went into timeless penance to get free from the sin of killing a son of Brahmana. Earth started facing major natural calamities in the absence of Indra, the ruler of Gods. To solve this matter, all gods and rishis decided to appoint Nahusha as the lord of heavens. Nahusha being less powerful and feeble, received a boon from rishis that, whichever creature comes in the radius within his sight, whether that being a God, a Rakshasa, an Asura, a Rishi, a Yaksha, a Gandharva, or a Pitri, he will absorb that being's power and grow strong. Thus, having derived a great power and strength, Nahusha became arrogant and started indulging in sensual pleasures by exploiting heavenly enjoyments. And once, while he was enjoying himself, his sight fell upon Sachi, Indra's wife. Allured by her beauty, he started persuading her to become his queen. Sachi was firmly reluctant. She took refuge of god's preceptor Brihaspati. Brihaspati assured her that Nahusha will not retain his power. Sachi also worshipped goddess Night to reach Indra who was in a minute form doing severe austerities as part of repentance. Sachi met Indra and seek his advice. Having consulted and taken his suggestion, Sachi came to Nahusha and said, 'O Nahusha, I will accept to be your queen, but I have a condition. Indra had possession of horses for transporting him, and also elephants, and chariots. I want you to have as a king of the gods, a unique vehicle, such once never possessed by any god or a being. Let many numbers of accomplished rishis carry you in a palanquin.' Nahusha immediately deployed to his celestial palanquin many sages like brahma rishis and royal rishis devoted to the asceticism. Out of intoxication of power and arrogance, he commanded those great sages to bear his palanquin. The holy souled Brahmanas and divine saints, while transporting him, got tired and questioned him, 'O king of gods, Vedas prescribed some definite hymns, administered to be recited while sprinkling the cows. Are those hymns genuine or not? Nahusha, who had lost his reasons due to conduct of vile acts, told them that those were not genuine.' The divine saints then said, 'You are taking path of sinfulness. The greatest sages have formerly said these hymns are authentic.' And out of arrogance, Nahusha touched Agastya Rishi's head with his foot. Enraged Agastya rishi spoke to him, 'Since you have defiled the holy hymns of the Veda and because you have contacted my head with your foot, and also you have turned these inaccessible rishis, equal to Brahma, into beasts for transporting you, hence, you will lose all your luster and will have fall from heaven, due to exhaustion of your meritorious deeds. You will turn into gigantic snake roaming on the earth and will remain in this form for ten thousand years. When this period is over, you will be able to come back to heaven.' This is how King Nahusha lost his throne in the heaven & hurled towards earth in the form of giant snake.

Many thousand years passed, once Pandavas during the forest exile made a stop at the hermitage of Vrishaparva, in the Himalayan mountains and forests. Bhima deciding to venture into the forest started his expedition on the foot, after several hours of roaming in the forest, he noticed a serpent of massive proportions, living and covering the whole cave with its mass. And spotting Bhima coming very close to him, the snake suddenly got provoked and goat-devouring serpent fiercely clutched him in his grasp. On account of the boon possessed by (Nahusha) in the former times, Bhimasena having his body in the serpent's clutch, quickly exhausted all his power. Armed Bhima, though endowed with immense physical power struggled desperately to rescue himself without any success.

Bhima asked, 'O snake, who are you? What are you going to do with me? I am Bhimasena, the son of Pandu, immediate brother of Yudhishthira. I carry the power of elephants, ten thousand in numbers, how are you able to subdue me?'

Snake replied, 'You must have heard about the royal sage, Nahusha the son of King Ayu, and the extender of the lineage of your forebears. I am that same one. For having insulted the sages, I, by (effect of) Agastya's curse have reached to this condition. You are from my blood line so you must not be slain by me, yet today I will swallow you! When I was descending from heaven, I urged to that reverent sage (Agastya), 'Please discharge me from this curse.' Having mercy upon me, Agastya told me, 'O king, you shall be released from the curse after some time is elapsed. That man who has a knowledge of the association existing between the Soul and the Supreme Being and could be able to meet the queries posed by you, shall liberate you.'

As Bhima did not return even after whole day has passed, and sensing bad omens, Yudhishthira started from his hermitage in the search of Bhima. In the thick forest near the cave, Yudhishthira discovering his dear brother wounded around by the flesh of a great snake, he uttered, 'O Bhima, how did you fall into this misfortune! And who is that supreme serpent with a body similar to a mountain pile?' Bhimasena said, 'O reverent one, this ferocious serpent has entrapped me for food. In the incarnation of snake, he is the king and royal sage Nahusha.' Yudhishthira urged, 'O long-lived one, liberate my brother of boundless bravery, we will offer you other food that will feed your hunger.' The serpent said, 'Now, I have caught this prince as a meal, which came to my mouth by himself. You should go away. You must not stay here.' Yudhishthira again asked, 'By getting what or by grasping what will you obtain contentment, O snake, and what meal shall I offer you?' Snake replied, 'O pure soul, I am your ancient ancestor, I am the son of King Ayu and from the moon, fifth in order of lineage. I was a king famed with a name, Nahusha. And by oblations, asceticism, self-control and mastering the Veda, I had gained a permanent supremacy all over the three worlds. And when I had attained the throne of Indra, arrogance possessed me. However, if today, you are able to answer well all the questions asked by me, then I will free Bhima!' Hearing these words, Yudhishthira said, 'O serpent, question anything you want to hear! I will answer your questions to please you! You have complete knowledge of what is essential to be known by Brahmanas (person of wisdom). Hence O lord of snakes, after hearing your queries, I shall answer!'

The snake said, 'O Yudhishthira, tell me--Who is a Brahmana and what is necessary to be known? Through your oration, I assume you to be extremely intelligent.'

Yudhishthira answered, 'O supreme amongst serpents, he, in whom we find truth, charity, mercy, superior conduct, kindness, adherence of the rites of his order and compassionate is a Brahmana. And, O serpent, the Supreme Being (Para Brahma), is the one which is necessary to be known, in that there is neither joy nor misery and after attaining it, the beings are not afflicted by the misery; what is your point of view?'

The serpent said, 'O King Yudhishthira, all these virtues and the Veda works for the good of the four classes in the society and are observed indeed in the Sudra and not only in Brahmana. And regarding the object to be known, you said, it is lacking both joy and misery, but I do not view any such object which does not have both.'

Yudhishthira said, 'Those attributes that are prevail in a Sudra, do not found in a Brahmana; neither those which are in a Brahmana, found in a Sudra. By birth alone, neither Sudra is a Sudra nor Brahmana is a Brahmana. It is

stated by the wise that person that has these qualities is a Brahmana. And although he is a Brahmana by birth, he is termed as a Sudra which does not have these qualities. And your word that there is no such object which exist which lacks both joy and misery. Like as in cold, heat is not present, nor in heat, the cold, so it gives no entity in which both (joy and sorrow) cannot exist?'

The serpent replied, 'O king, if you define Brahmana by attributes then the difference of caste turns worthless till the character and conduct do come into picture.'

Yudhishthira said, 'O powerful snake, in human civilization, it is tough to confirm one's caste, due to undiscriminating intercourse among the four classes. This is my point of view. Men affiliated to all classes promiscuously father offspring from women of all the classes. And for human, birth, speech, sexual intercourse and death, these phenomena are common. That is why at the opening ceremony of a sacrificial rites, Rishis use expressions as- whatever caste we shall belong to, we perform the sacrifice. Therefore, the wise people have confirmed that "Character" is the key necessity. O excellent snake! Whosoever now satisfy the rules of virtuous and moral conduct, him I have termed as a Brahmana.'

The serpent responded, "O Yudhishthira, you are fully conversant of judicious knowledge and after listening your speech, how can I now swallow your brother!"

Yudhishthira asked, "You are so knowledgeable in the Vedas and Vedangas; so, narrate me, what one must perform to attain salvation?"

The serpent replied, 'O descendent of Bharata, I hold the opinion that the man which gives charity on appropriate subjects, says kind words and always speaks the truth and refrains from doing harm to any creature, attains to heaven.'

Yudhishthira asked, 'Which is the significant of the two, truth or charity? Advise me also on the greater or smaller significance of kind words and of abstaining from doing harm to any creature.'

The snake replied, 'The comparative significance of these virtues depends on its purpose or utility. Truth is sometimes more worthy as compared to acts of alms giving; some of the charities are more worthy than true speech. Similarly, abstaining from doing harm to any creature is observed as more significant than kind words and vice-versa. So, it depends on its effect. And O Yudhishthira, if you have anything at all to inquire, express it, I shall explain you!'

Yudhishthira inquired, 'O snake, explain me how the spiritual being's movement to celestial heavens, its awareness by the sensory organs and its happiness of the unchangeable fruits of its actions, can be understood.'

The great snake replied, 'On account of his own deeds, man is noticed to have attained one of the three qualifications of human living life in a heaven or takes birth in the nether regions. Out of them, a person who is not lethargic, who do not cause injury to anyone and the one who is dignified with generosity and different virtuous qualities, departs to celestial regions, after exiting the earth. But by acting the opposite, people are born as human beings or as lower form of animals. In this regard, it is specially said, that a man who is influenced by anger, lust, greed, and malice degrades from his human birth and takes birth again as a lower form of animal, and even those lower form of animals too could get birth into the human state; and the elephant, cow, horse and some animals are noticed to have attain the celestial state. O my son, thus earning the fruits of one's deeds, the living being thus reincarnate through these different states; but the person of wisdom rests his soul in the eternal Supreme Soul. The incarnate spirit, confined by fate and obtaining the fruits of its deeds, experiences successive births, one after another, but the one that do not have any association with his acts (renunciation of karmas), is aware of the unchangeable fate of all beings that are born.'

Yudhishthira inquired, "O snake, let me know the truth and without ambiguity, how that disconnected spirit becomes aware of senses like sound, touch, form, hear and taste. O great-minded, 'Do you not comprehend them, at the same time by the senses?'"

The snake replied, 'O Yudhishthira, the Atman (spirit), applying itself in a mortal body and showing itself via the sense organs, becomes properly conscious of visible objects. O prince, the mind, and the intellect, the senses, helping the soul to perceive objects, are known as Karanas.'

Yudhishthira said, 'Reveal me the differentiating attributes of the mind and the intellect. For the person meditating on Supreme Soul, this knowledge is declared as the main duty.'

The serpent replied, 'It is due to illusion, the soul becomes slave to the intellect. The intellect, although a subservient of the soul, becomes the director of it. The intellect plays itself by acts of perception; the mind is self-determined. The Intellect is not the source of the sensation (like sight, hearing, flavors, smell) but the mind is. These are the differentiating factors between the mind and the intellect, my son. As you too have knowledge in this regard, what is your point of view?'

Yudhishthira said, 'O most learned one, you have marvelous intellect, and you have complete knowledge of what is appropriate to be known. Why do you pose me that question? You have all knowledge and you had also performed great deeds, to be lived and rule the heaven. How did the illusion overpower you? This is my biggest doubt.'

The snake replied, 'Success and wealth intoxicates even the intelligent and brave men. People living in affluence, lose their rational mind. I too went through the same. O Yudhishthira, captivated by the obsession of riches, I have descended from my high position and now having regained my identity, am enlightening you thus! O triumphant king, you have done good to me. Having conversation of righteous like you, my painful curse is vanished.'

After uttering this, the king, Nahusha, left his serpentine avatar, and by retaking his celestial form he traveled back to heaven. The illustrious and righteous Yudhishthira also came back to his forest retreat with his brother and family priest Dhaumya.

8

Kausika and The Virtuous Fowler

In Aranyaka Parva of Mahabharata, there is another enchanting story told by Sage Markandeya to Yudhishthira about a spiritual dialogue between Brahmana named Kausika and a virtuous fowler from Mithila. This story here is a small excerpt of that dialog which delves upon the path to supreme salvation. The story follows like this-

There was a virtuous hermit by name Kausika, he was scholar and dedicated to the learning of the Vedas, Vedangas, and the Upanishads. Once while sitting at the pedestal of a tree, out of nowhere a female crane sitting on the peak befouled on the Brahmana's body. Noticing this act by crane the Brahmana became very angry and started contemplating of injuring her. As soon as the Brahmana looked furiously at the crane, she dropped dead on the earth. Watching her falling and insensible, the Brahmana was deeply moved by compassion filled with pity and began to bemoan saying, 'Oh, I have committed such a foul deed, motivated by anger and malice!'

Moksha - The Immortal Bliss

After muttering these words again and again, that learned Brahmana went into a village for collecting alms. He visited several houses of persons of fine descent taking alms, the Brahmana came to one house with who he was acquainted before. Reaching that house, he said, 'Give'. And he was answered by house lady, 'Stay'. And when that housewife got engaged in preparing a cleaned vessel in which the alms would be given, her husband unexpectedly barged into the house in hungry state. The virtuous housewife attended her husband immediately and ignoring the Kausika, she first extended her husband some water to clean his feet and face and then provided a seat and after that she served him tasty meal and drink, by humbly waiting beside him in order to pay attention to all his needs. She always acted what was agreeable and kind with her husband. She was also with full devout worshipping the gods and the needs of visitors and aides, and also her in-law parents.

While attending her husband, suddenly her eyes captured the Brahmana, she recalled that she had told him to wait for the alms. She felt very ashamed and immediately took alms, for giving it to the waiting Brahmana. Looking at her angrily, the Brahmana said, 'I am shocked at your conduct! having requested me to 'Stay,' you didn't dismiss me!'

Seeing the Brahmana filled with fumes and bursting with anger, that virtuous woman started soothing his temper and said, 'O learned one, it is appropriate for you to pardon me. My husband is my foremost god. He came home hungry and exhausted, hence got served attentively by me.' Listening to her, the Brahmana said, 'For you, Brahmanas are not deserving the better treatment. Do you consider your spouse greater than them?' listening to what that

Brahmana said, the woman replied, 'I am no she-crane, O ascetic! You are blessed with the distinguished wealth of asceticism, leave your anger. I do not disrespect Brahmanas, possessing with a highly virtuous souls, they are equivalent to gods themselves. But this mistake of mine, it suits you to forgive. I appreciate the spirit and greatness of ascetic Brahmanas having knowledge and wisdom. O holy one, you are well familiar of virtue, righteousness, and devoted to studying of the Vedas. However, I think you do not know what actually the "virtue" is. Travel to the town of Mithila, ask there for a virtuous fowler. You are not actually conversant with what highest virtue stands for. In Mithila, you will find a fowler, who adheres to the path of truth, honest and steadfast in servicing his parents and he has full restraint over his senses. Even he will lecture you on virtue. After listening all this from a righteous woman, the Brahmana replied, 'I am pleased with you. God bless you; my anger has almost vanished, O beautiful one! The criticism by you will be of the most beneficial to me.'

Constantly thinking upon the speech of that woman, Kausika started criticizing himself and in a guilty feeling thought about subtle path of righteousness and virtue, he murmured himself, 'I must agree with all the due respect what woman has told and should travel to Mithila.'

His trust in that lady was strengthened by her awareness of the incident of she-crane's death and her words about the essence of virtue. Kausika once again contemplated with admiration of all what that woman said and then with a curious mind started his journey to Mithila. He traveled through many forests, villages and cities and finally reached Mithila, ruled by King Janaka.

In the town, after enquiring few denizens, Brahmana spotted the fowler sitting in a butcher's patio, that ascetic fowler was busy in trading buffalo meat. As the large crowd of meat-buyers assembled around the fowler, Kausika kept waiting at a distance. Noticing that Brahmana, Fowler immediately left his seat, and approached him, the fowler said, 'I greet you, O sacred one! You are welcome, you are best of Brahmanas! I am the fowler. Order me, how may I help you? the word that the virtuous woman said to you, 'Travel to Mithila,' I am aware of it. I am also aware for what purpose you have come here in Mithila.' Brahmana was taken aback, after hearing these words from fowler. He babbled to himself, 'This is definitely the second wonder that I experienced!' After a while, the fowler told to Brahmana, 'This area in which you are now standing is not appropriate for you, if it is acceptable to you, let us pay visit to my house, O pure souled one!'

After this, both proceeded to the home of fowler. By revering the guest arrived at his home, fowler extended him a seat and provided water to clean his face and feet. The Brahmana accepted this with great pleasure, occupied his seat and then spoke to the fowler, 'In my view, this profession of yours does not suit you. O fowler, I feel sorry that you follow such a cruel profession.' Hearing this the fowler replied, 'This is a family profession, I have inherited it from my father and grandfathers. O Brahmana do not feel sorry for me as I am merely sticking to the duties that came to me by birth. By fulfilling the duties assigned in my destiny by the creator, I diligently serve elders and teachers. O you finest of Brahmanas! I always utter the truth, never carry envy for others and give best of my abilities. O Brahmana, my profession is to trade pork and buffalo meat without butchering these animals by myself, but that are killed by others. I feel satisfied living upon whatever remains after first offering it to the deities, visitors, and dependents. I strictly abstain from saying ill about anyone, be that thing be little or great. The actions of past lives all the time follow its actor.'

Having heard this speech of the fowler, the Brahmana having excellent wisdom, questioned the fowler, 'How do I know what is the virtuous conduct? You are eminent amongst virtuous men, therefore O exalted soul, reveal to me about it truly. To answer this question, the fowler replied, "O finest amongst Brahmanas, Sacrifices (ritual offerings or yagna), Charity (gift giving or dana), Asceticism (controlling sensual pleasures) the Vedas (holy scriptures) and Truth (spiritual reality) - these five pure objects that are any time present in the conduct is called virtuous. Conquering lust, anger, pride, greed, and deceit, they that take pleasure in virtue because it is virtue, are considered as truly virtuous. Such persons deserve the recognition as virtuous. Between this person who is virtuous and the person who is dedicated to sacrificial rites & and learning of the Vedas, there is no difference. They both follow the path of the truth and the righteousness, which is indeed a second quality of virtuous. The core spirit of the Vedas is Truth: the spirit of Truth is self-restraint, and the spirit of self-restraint is abstinence from the sensual and material pleasures of the world. These all attributes are found in the conduct of that is virtuous."

After a deatiled discourse on virtuousness, further question was asked by Kausika on the spiritual matter which leads to explaining the attainment to supreme goal of human life, a salvation.

The virtuous fowler further explains to Brahman, "A pure-minded person, having purified his soul, is successful in destroying both the good and bad consequences of his deeds and therefore he could attain the everlasting bliss through the awareness of his inner spirit. Achieving the state of tranquility and enlightenment is like a person who in a happy condition of mind sleeps soundly. By fasting and following strict regimen of food, such a pure-minded person grasps the Supreme Spirit mirrored in his own. By exercising the deep meditation in the evening and small hours of the night, he contemplates on the Supreme Soul which is beyond any qualities and in the illuminated heart, glimmering like a bright beacon and therefore he obtains salvation.

Greed and anger should be crushed by all means; because this act contains the holiest virtue that people can exercise and is considered as a best mean by which person can pass through to the other end of this sea of trouble and tribulations. A person must safeguard his virtuousness from getting suffered by the vicious effects of anger, his virtues from the influence of ego and pride, his wisdom from the fallout of arrogance and his inner soul from the illusion.

Compassion and mercy are the greatest of attributes, and self-control is the greatest of powers, the knowing self-spiritual nature is the greatest of all knowledge, and truthfulness is the greatest of all religious duties.

Knowledge and observance of truth is admirable, but what contributes to the greatest benefit of all creatures, is known as the highest truth. The one who performs action not with an objective of getting reward or blessing, but who has renounced everything as per the needs of his renunciation, is a true Sannyasin and is truly wise person. And as union with supreme soul cannot be instructed, even by our spiritual gurus--he only provides us a hint to the enigma. Renunciation of the physical things or material world is known as Yoga. We must never harm and avenge any living being and always live in peace and harmony with all. Self-renunciation, relinquishment of desires, and peaceful composed mind- these are the methods using which one can secure spiritual enlightenment; and the self-knowledge (one's inner soul's nature) is the greatest of all knowledge. The Muni (ascetic) who aspires to attain moksha (salvation), which is extremely difficult to achieve, must be continuously occupied in austerities, patient, self-controlled and should sacrifice that passion and attachment which ties him to the material and physical objects of the world. They name all these the qualities of the HIM, the Supreme Soul. The gunas (worldly qualities and attributes) that are known to us, gets reduced down to agunas (non-gunas) in HIM. Supreme Soul is not constrained by anything and can be comprehended by the growth and evolution of our spiritual vision. Moment the deception of ignorance is disappeared, this "Supreme Bliss" is attained. By avoiding both the objects of joy and sorrow and by forsaking the emotions and desires which tie up him to the worldly objects, a person may obtain Brahma (merging with Supreme Soul or attainment of liberation)."

When all these deep mysteries of salvation was revealed to that Brahmana, he became extremely happy and he said to the fowler, "All that is explained by you, is enlightened, as it is impossible for a person born as a fowler to discover the enigmas of the immortal religion (sanatan dharma), I regard you not to be so. For sure, there should be some secret in relation with your past karma. I would like to know the reality in this matter."

The fowler responded, "O fine Brahmana, there exists a story of my previous birth. In the former birth, I was Brahmana too, learned in the Vedas and Vedangas. I had a friendship with King skilled in the branch of archery, from his company, I acquired expertise in archery. One day the king, ventured out on a hunting excursion, me and all his ministers accompanied him. He killed many deer near an ashram (monastery) of a rishi. I too fired a terrible arrow, but that arrow hit one rishi and he was badly wounded with a fatal injury. He dropped down on the ground, with lot of pain and said, 'I never caused any harm to anyone, which wicked man has done this?' I told to that rishi who was laying on the ground, 'This caused by me unintentionally, please pardon my mistake.' But, O Brahmana, the rishi, cursed me in a fury, 'You shall be born as a cruel fowler.' I attempted to appease him saying, 'Forgive me, O muni, I committed this sinful act unintentionally. It befits you to forgive me. Venerable sir, calm yourself.' Over my pleas that rishi replied, 'The curse once uttered cannot be reversed. Although you will be born as fowler, you shall remain a religious devout man and you will surely honour your parents & elders and with this you will attain great spiritual perfection; you will also be able to remember the events of your last birth and attain heaven after the expiration of the curse, you will be again born as a Brahmana.'"

After hearing this story of fowler's previous birth, Brahmana said, "I consider any lower born who is graced with these virtues - uprightness, self-control, and truthfulness, as a Brahmana. A man grows into Brahmana by his character and not by birth; by his own evil actions, a man attains a sinful life and terrible downfall in the end. Farewell, O best of pious men, may you be successful, and may virtuousness guard you, and may you be steadfast in the practice of virtue." And that superior Brahmana circumambulated him and then left.

9

Bhagiratha and Salvation Giver Ganga

In Ramayana's Bala Kand, there is a story of Rama's ancestor, King Sagara, and his descendants. This tale recounts how holy river Ganga appeared on earth after the severe penances by Bhagiratha, and the sacred waters of her bestowing salvation to his ancestors and the many human generations that followed.

In very ancient times, there was a ruler of Ayodhya named King Sagara, who is ancestor of Lord Rama. He was childless and keenly desiring for children. Vidharbha's princess named Keshini, was the eldest wife of Sagara. And she was righteous and forthright. The second wife of Sagara, Sumati was the Arishtanemi's daughter and Suparna's sister, she was beautiful and charming.

Taking his queens together the powerful king of Ayodhya reached Himavat Mountain ranges and began to practice asceticism in the forest of Bhriguprasravana.

After a century passed, the great yogi Maharishi Brighu was delighted with Sagara's austerities & gave a boon saying, "O sinless one, you will be blessed with many sons, and you will attain fame unmatched among men. One of your queens will give a birth to a son which will extend your race and from the other wife, the sixty thousand sons (will be born)." Listening to what Maharishi Bhrigu said, both queens with clasped hands, asked, "O Brahmana, may your boon come true! Tell us, which one of us shall give a birth to a single son and who will give to many?"

Hearing this, the highly reverent Rishi Bhrigu said- "This will be as per your wish. Which one of you want to be mother of a single son, who will extend the dynasty and who desires to procreate sixty thousand powerful sons?"

Hearing the ascetic's words, Keshini prefers to choose a single son and Sumati, sixty thousand sons.

After paying obeisance to Maharishi, the king returned to his capital, accompanied by his queens. After a period of time elapsed, the elder queen, Keshini gave a birth to a son whose name was Asamanja. And Sumati, conceived to give a birth to fetus which was gourd shaped. And when it was opened up, sixty thousand sons emerged out. And the royal nurses took care of those sixty thousand sons by nurturing them in jars filled with clarified butter. A great period of time passed; they reached to the age of youth. The eldest son Asamanjasa often used to grab those children and flung them into the Sharayu River, taking evil pleasure from this mean act. Having such evil tendency and also harming and injuring innocent people and citizens, he was forced into exile by his father King Sagara, from the city. And Asamanja had a very brave son named Anshuman, adored by all citizens and he gave due respect and courtesy to every person.

After many years passed, King Sagara took up the decision of performing a sacrifice. High priests of king initiated sacrificial rites by chanting Vedas hymns.

The region between Himavat and the Vindhya is where the King Sagara performed this sacrifice, as this land was best fitting as a sacrificial ground. Skilled archer and brave fighter, Prince Anshuman was selected as a protector of the horse of the sacrifice. Aiming to interrupt the sacrifice of the monarch, one day Vasava, took the guise of a Rakshasi and sneaked away the sacrificial horse. All the priests engaged in rites ceremony approached the king and urged, 'On such an auspicious occasion, someone has snatched the sacrificial horse by violence. O King, kill that horse stealer and get back the horse, else the sacrifice will be faulty and bring us great misfortune.'

After hearing the cries of priests, Sagara called all his sixty thousand sons and addressed to his court, saying, 'In such a great sacrifice as this, sanctified by mantras and executed by extremely divine priests, I do not understand how Rakshasas may accessed it. Therefore, look for the horse, my sons. May Good befall you! Search the entire earth enclosed by the seas and dig out till the sacrificial horse is found on my command. As I have started these sacrificial rites, I cannot leave the ceremony. Proceed, my sons! I would remain present here with my grandsons and priests.' Thus, as ordained by the King Sagara, his princes happily started the searching expedition of the horse. They crossed the entire world but without the success of finding that horse, they commenced the work of digging the ground using their hands resembling thunderbolts. They used ploughs and other tools to excavate the earth, the earth trembled with the sound. Many serpents, and Asuras, and Rakshasas, and other creatures were injured and slaughtered. They excavated the earth, till the lowest depths of underground. In the search for the horse, the sons of Sagara pierced the Jambudwipa, filled with mountains. All the deities, along with Gandharvas, Asuras and Nagas alarmed, reached before Lord Brahma, bowing before the Lord with the distressed and torments, they said: O Venerable Lord, the whole earth has been dug up by the sons of Sagara and caused sufferings and death to many innocent beings. If anyone opposes them is wounded by these words, "You are a stealer, you have poached the sacrificial horse."

Hearing the pleas from them, Lord Brahma said, "This whole earth belongs to great Vasudeva, as she is being her consort. And that enchanting one is in fact her lord. In the form of Sage Kapila, he endlessly supports the earth. The sons of King Sagara will be swallowed by his raging fire." Hearing those words of Lord Brahma, all gods returned to their worlds, in joyous spirit.

Meantime, the tumult created by Sons of Sagara by excavating the earth raised a ferocious noise like thunderous bolt. After traversing the whole world, those princes returned back to their father and said, "We have combed the entire earth and slain danavas, rakshas, pishachas, snakes and gods, but we could not find either the horse or the thief. O Father, what are we to do next? May excellence be with you, please give us further instructions after considering this matter."

The King Sagara replied in wrath, "Do it again and dig the earth, search the horse and be successful in your objective, and having caught the thief of the horse, cease." In pursuit of his royal command, those sixty thousand sons of King Sagara renewed their excavation and in the depths of earth they came across a great monstrous size elephant named Virupaksha who resembled same as a mountain. The whole earth and its mountains and forests were supported on the head of this mighty elephant & when due to fatigue the elephant shakes his head to relax himself, then the entire earth shakes and trembles with the earthquake. The princes bowed before him and went round that elephant by giving respects. Then they continued piercing the underground, having excavated east, they excavated south and in southern region, they witnessed the second mighty elephant named Mahapadma, looking like a mountain supporting the earth. They offered him honors and homage.

Then those brave sons of Sagara, started piercing western region and there they behold the elephant of the western region named Saumanasa appearing like a gigantic mountain after circumambulating him and giving respects, they reached at the northern region. While digging up northern region of the earth, they found a white elephant that appeared like the snow mountain. He is called as Himapandara & he stood like colossal supporting that part of the earth. And having paid honors and going round him those sixty thousand princes went on further, piercing the depths of the earth. Then those brave and mighty sons of Sagara penetrated the earth reaching to the famous quarter of north-eastern region. Here they witnessed the immortal Lord Vasudeva in the incarnating form of Shri Kapila. And to their immense pleasure, they found the sacrificial horse grazing in his vicinity. Thinking that Shri Kapila had abducted the horse, those furious warriors, in full of wrath carrying ploughs, bearing spades and countless tress and rocks, attacked him, shouting: 'Stay there! you are the thief of the sacrificial horse, you are caught into the hands of the sons of King Sagara.' Having heard those words, engulfed with rage, Shri Kapila roared tremendously with the sound 'H'm, and instantly the sons of Sagara were burned to the ashes by all-powerful Kapila.

Looking at very long period that has passed since the mission of his sons and delays of their return, King Sagara addressed his courageous and powerful grandson Anshuman, 'O Child, you are heroic and distinguished like your ancestors, go, and find out the well-being of your uncles and search the horse thief also. Since there are mighty creatures and beings inhabiting the earth's inner region, do take your bow and sword. If you encounter those who deserved to be worshipped, pay your respects in reverence, and slay those who obstructs you. After accomplishing your goal, return back and contribute to the completion of my sacrifice.'

As per King Sagara's command, Anshuman armed himself with bow and sword and immediately departed. He discovered the underground route that is dug up by his uncles. On this route, he came across the extremely powerful and gigantic elephant of cardinal direction, who was worshipped by deities and danavas, asuras, nagas, pishachas, goblins, birds, and serpents. After going round of him, Anshuman bowed in respect and asked about his welfare. He asked about his uncles and thief. Listening to those enquiries, the powerful elephant answered- 'O Son of

Asamanja, you will successfully achieve your objective and soon return to the capital with the horse.'

Anshuman continued his journey further and by each turn, enquired with the same question to each of all the elephants supporting other cardinal directions. Each time after paying respects to them, he was asked by elephants to continue further. Advised by them, he come to a place where his uncles had been burned down to heaps of ashes. Heavy with a grief, sorrowful Anshuman wept after seeing their deadly destruction. Stricken with agony and distress, Anshuman suddenly notices the horse grazing in vicinity. Wishful of carrying out the rites with offering of water oblation for his departed uncles, looked around but did not find the water nearby. While looking at far, he saw the maternal uncle, Suparna, the lord of birds and holy eagle, who addressed Anshuman, saying, "O foremost of men, do not lament, the carnage of these princes was for the welfare of everyone. These powerful ones have been reduced to the ashes by the Great Kapila of incredible majesty. Therefore, it is not suitable to offer the normal rites for them. O supreme among men, perform your uncle's rites with the waters of holy river Ganga who is a first daughter of Himalayas. As the waters of that purifier of the world, the holy Ganga would stream forth their ashes, the rites will be successful, and sixty thousand princes will attain celestial heaven. Now you go back by taking this horse and accomplish the sacrificial rites of your grandfather."

Glorious and powerful Prince Anshuman, after listening to the speech of Suparna, left immediately for the capital by taking the horse. Approaching the King Sagara, who was awaiting the completion of sacrificial rites communicated the words of Holy eagle, Suparna. The king properly accomplished the sacrifice as per the scriptures and returned back to his capital, but the king did not find any ways and means by which he can cause holy Ganga to descend on the earth. And after ruling for thirty thousand years, he ascended heaven without accomplishing the matter of devising a way to bring Ganga.

Upon the death of king Sagara, ministers appointed Anshuman as their king. Anshuman proved as a great Monarch. His successor, his son, the Dilipa, was also a great king. Installing Dilipa in his kingdom, Anshuman began severe austerities on the summit of the Himalayas. After thirty-two thousand years passed and living on austerities in the forest, without able to achieve any means by which sacred Ganga to descend on the earth, he passed away.

That mighty ruler Dilipa was afflicted with sorrow when acquainted with account of the destruction of great uncles & still he could not devise any course about it. He always pondered on the ways that he could make this descent of the Great Ganga possible, so as to perform the final rites for the salvation of his forebears.

King Dilipa was blessed with exceptionally virtuous son named Bhagiratha. King Dilipa ruled for thirty thousand years, and during his reign, he performed many sacrifices. But he too could not reach to any decision on how to deliver salvation to his ancestors. Having caught with illness, breathed his last. After coronation of his son Bhagiratha as a king, his spirit ascended to abode of Indra.

Bhagiratha was possessed of great virtue & royal sage. He had no children and, in the desire, to obtain a son, he consigned the administration of kingdom to his counsellors and went to holy place called Gokarna where he observed yogic penances to bring down the holy Ganga. Controlling his senses, eating only once a month, and standing in the middle of five fires, and with arms uplifted. Thousand years thus passed while he was performing terrible austerities.

Lord Brahma and ruler of the universe was pleased with Bhagiratha and appeared together with other devas, they approached highly virtuous king Bhagiratha and said: "O Bhagiratha, your righteous and ardent yogic practices deserve our commendation; ask for a book, O blesses One."

The glowing Bhagiratha, with clasped hands bowed in reverence to Shri Brahma and said, "O blessed Lord, if you are delighted to grant the fruits of my austerities then bestow on me a boon that, may King Sagara's sons get offering of water through my hands, and the ashes of them flown by the holy stream of Ganga and with that may my great-grand-fathers reach to heaven. And, O Lord, I pray you that Ishwaku dynasty never suffers for the desire of offspring, I be blessed with an heir."

After King Bhagiratha prayed for this, Grandsire addressed him in soft and gratifying words- 'O mighty king Bhagiratha, you have very high and noble purpose. May it happen so! And let your wish for a son be realized. O king, this Ganga, Himavat's eldest daughter, descends on the earth with enormous force, so to maintain her pray to Lord Shiva. O king, earth will not be able to bear the great force applied by her sharp fall."

After addressing this to King Bhagiratha and by offering salutations to Ganga, Lord Brahma and other gods departed to their own celestial abodes.

When Lord Brahma had departed, Bhagiratha, worshipped Lord Shiva in standing pose, by compressing the earth surface with the tip of the toe, spent a full year thus in Lord's adoration. When one year was over, Uma's Lord Pashupati Mahadeva venerated by the whole world, appeared, and spoke to King saying- "O Illustrious one, I am pleased by your worship, I will fulfill your desire, I will hold the descent of Ganga on my head."

Then after, that one who is revered by all creatures, the first daughter of Himavat took the enormous form of river and with torrential impact precipitated on the Siva's head. Celestial Ganga thought- I will press the Lord Mahadeva to enter the nether regions, by carrying him with my mighty streams. Lord Shiva knowing her thoughts, became angry and determined to arrest her flow into locks of his hair. As majestic as Himalayas, the locks of Lord Shiva hold her falling and the holy river got imprisoned in tangled locks. For many years, wandering around there and despite her innumerable attempts Ganga could not find egress from the matted locks of Shiva. Having noticed divine river's plight, Shri Bhagiratha entered into severe austerities and penances to please the Lord Shiva again. Consequently, extremely pleased Lord Shiva let loose the Ganga off in the course of Vindu Lake. And when she fell her flow was divided into seven streams. The three streams of sacred waters Hladini, Pavani and Nalini flowed in the direction of east from the head of Lord Shiva, while holy waters in other three streams named the Sindhu, the Sita, and the Suchakshu the flowed towards auspicious west.

And the seventh followed King Bhagiratha's chariot. Riding on a stunning chariot, the royal sage Bhagiratha proceeded, and the divine river Ganga followed him. Thus, the holiest river took a plunge from celestial heavens up on the head of

Lord Shiva and therefrom came flowing on the earth. Her fall generated tremendous thunderous sound. The earth looked charming with the throng of falling creatures like fishes, tortoises, and porpoises. To witness such an auspicious event of Ganga's descent on the earth, gods, and saints, gandharvas, yakshas and siddhas mounted on magnificent elephants and horses and chariots as big as cities, descended upon the earth.

In their divine chariot Pariplava, the gods flocked to see this marvelous event, the luster of their celestial ornaments illuminated the cloudless sky as if thousand suns are shining upon the earth.

The spirited fishes, porpoises and serpents leaping from stream sparkled like lightening in the sky, while foam and sprinkles dispersed on all sides, appearing like winter clouds swarmed with cranes and swans.

Pure waters of holy Ganga sometimes gushed rapidly, sometimes bent, sometimes in magnitude, sometimes rising up in the air, sometimes slow, sometimes dashing against rocks, sometimes ascending up and then falling on the land. This sacred water capable of removing sin, captivated the minds while running on the plains of the earth. The sages, gandharvas, and the dwellers of the earth, touched the holy water streaming from Lord Shiva's matted hair.

And those that were cursed and fallen from the heaven on to the earth, after having bathed in Ganga waters, they were freed from the sins by bathing in hallowed water. These beings again returned to the respective regions of heaven. All the regions wherever that pure water flowed, all beings cheered and having dipped in Ganga, became cleansed from the sin.

Moksha - The Immortal Bliss

Riding on the excellent chariot the mighty king and the royal sage Bhagiratha, drove on and Ganga followed after him. And the gods, the sages, the rakshasas, the asuras, the danavas, gandharvas, yakshas, and the Kinnaras, and the mighty serpents and the Apsaras, the aquatic animals, all took part as confluence witnessing holy Ganga. And wherever king Bhagiratha took his chariot, the celebrated Ganga, supreme of all streams, power of destroying all sins, flowed. Thus, while flowing, Shri Ganga reached the sacrificial ground of the Rishi Jahnu, and flooded the place while he was performing a sacrifice. The Rishi Jahnu recognizing the arrogance of river, grew angry and by enlarging his body drank up all her sublime waters. The gods, the gandharvas, and the celestial sages were amazed with this miracle and began worshipping Rishi Jahnu, they proclaimed, "From this day the holy river will be called as your daughter." And thus, vigorous Rishi being pleased, let Ganga come off through his ears. From there on, holy river Ganga is also known as Jahnu's daughter, Jahnavi.

Finally, the holy waters of Ganga reached the ocean and penetrated the lower regions. The royal sage Bhagiratha diligently brought Ganga to the location at which sons of Sagara were burned to ashes, he looked at those ashes of his ancestor with a grief. The exquisite waters of Ganga flowed over the heap of ashes; sons of Sagara attained salvation, with their sins purged, attained heaven.

Lord Brahma, the lord of all beings appeared and addressed the King Bhagiratha, "O powerful among men, the sixty thousand sons of King Sagara, have been redeemed and they attained celestials like the gods themselves. And, O king, as long as waters of the ocean remain on the earth,

Sagara's sons would dwell in heaven like divine beings. From now on, this Ganga will become famous as your eldest daughter and will be called after your name. This holy river will be called as Shri Ganga, Tripathaga and Bhagirathi. She is known as Tripathaga due to her course into three directions. O King, execute the funeral rites of your ancestors and perform this prescribed duty. The mighty king Sagara could not achieve this objective and Anshuman of infinite power failed to accomplish the sacred desire. Your father Dilipa equal to the gods in virtuous merit and brave warrior could not succeed in bringing down Ganga as per his resolution. That promise is now accomplished by you, you would achieve the eternal fame and praise in the entire world. And, O destroyer of your enemies, having brought Ganga on the earth, with this act you will attain the abodes of Brahma. O best amongst men, now you bathe in this holy water, purify yourself, and attain sanctity and virtuous deeds. And then carry out the watery rituals of your ancestor. O King, may you get the well-being and prosperity, return, and rule your capital, I will now leave to my abode."

Then the grandfather of all beings, Lord Brahma departed to his celestial region. And the royal sage king Bhagiratha after taking the holy bath in sacred waters of Ganga, offered waters to his ancestors and sons of Sagara. After returning to his capital, earning immense prosperity, the monarch ruled his kingdom, the people celebrated with jubilation and no longer suffered sorrows and miseries and with the well-being attained they could live in peace and harmony.

10

Kamagita: Krishna's advice to Yudhishthira

This story is about a situation after the end of Mahabharata war and find its mention in the section of Ashvamedha Parva.

When the great war of Mahabharata was over after the span of eighteen days, in Kurukshetra, there was a great carnage ever recorded in the short span of time. The king Yudhishthira even after winning this war against Kauravas, was in a great distress. With his senses disoriented, eyes overflowing with tears, he ascended the bank of the Ganga like an injured elephant pierced by the hunter. Yudhishthira, the son of Dharma, in a depressed and somber mood sat on the ground and sobbed again and again. Witnessing the king is in downcast state and helpless, the Pandavas engulfed with anguish, surrounded him.

Krishna saw the King Yudhishthira, distressed due to bereft of his kins and relatives slain in the war, Yudhishthira was appearing dejected like an eclipsed sun or fire stifled by the smoke. Lord Krishna comforting the son of Dharma, addressed him -

Vasudeva said, "O descendant of Bharata's race, salvation is not attained by giving up the external things like (possessions, valuables, kingdom etc.) it is only attained by giving up things which indulges to the physical body and senses. The virtue and happiness can be achieved by the renouncing the external things but if at the same time if the person is gripped by the desires and passions for bodily pleasure then consider it as our enemies.

The word with two letters is Mrit-yu (Death of the Soul), and the word with three letters is Sas-wa-ta (Eternal Soul) or Brahman. Mind's preoccupation that this or that thing belongs to me or the obsession to worldly objects is Mrityu and the absence of such a state of mind is Sas-wa-ta.

Both these Brahman and Mrityu, O King, have their home in the souls of living beings and cannot be seen; they fight battle with each other. And if, it is true that Eternal Soul is never destroyed, then one will never feel guilty of the death of a creature by piercing (killing) its physical body. What is important is having won the sovereignty of the entire earth with its movable and immovable things, he should not become attached to these things or get engrossed in its pleasure. If a man after renouncing the world, has become hermit in the forest, living on the raw food like wild roots and fruits, if such a man, has a desire and the addiction for good things of the world, he would bear Mrityu (death) in his self.

O Bharata, pay attention and observe the nature of your inner and outer enemies (with the spiritual practice), And the man who can visualize this nature of what is eternal truth is able to overreach the influence of the death.

Wise men do not seek an approval upon the conduct of those who are submerged in worldly pursuits, desires, and pleasures. There is no action without having desire and all desires are like the limbs of the mind.

Thus, such wise men who recognize this, conquer their desires. The Yogi who holds a close association with the Supreme Soul, is aware that Yoga is ultimate path (to liberation) due to the cause and effect of his action from many previous life births. And recalling from past births what the soul desires, is not going to help in achieving perfect devotion and virtue, but the control of all the desires is at the root of all true virtues. Such wise men avoid engaging in the custom of donation, learning Vedic scriptures and rites, observing asceticism and austerity, all these whose goal is the attainment of material prosperity or with the motive of securing any advantage thereby.

In order to explain of this truth, the sages who are familiar with the ancient knowledge, recite these poems known as "Kamagita" O Yudhishthira, listen to this poem in detail. In this Kama says, "There is no being in this world who can destroy me without the application of the appropriate means like, conquering of all desires and practice of Yoga etc." Kama states-

- If a man aware of my strength, seeks to destroy me by reciting prayers etc., I prevail over such man by deceiving him with the notion that I am the subjective and abstract ego within him.

- If he seeks to destroy me by using sacrificial rites with many offerings, I delude him by taking shape of most virtuous being in his mind, amongst all living beings (that is, by creating false ego in his mind).

- If he strives to root out me by learning the Vedas and Vedangas, I prevail over him by appearing in his mind as soul of virtue amongst all immovable things (that is, by creating delusion that he is most virtuous being ever).

- If the man with observance of truth, seek to overpower me by self-restraint, I take disguise of his own mind so that he cannot grasp my existence (as controller).

- If the man with observance of ascetic religious practices, seek to eradicate me with austerity, I take disguise of asceticism in his mind, and thus he is prevented from knowing me.

- And if the ignorant man thinks that learning and knowledge can eliminate me, to attain salvation (moksha), I prank and laugh in the face of such ignorant man.

- I am the eternal one without any peer or any comparison, whom no creature can kill or destroy.

Therefore, you too, O Prince Yudhishthira, redirect your desires (Kama) coming out of grief to Virtue, so that you could attain what is best suited for you now (after winning the great war of Mahabharata). Make arrangement for the execution of the horse sacrifice (Ashvamedha) with donations, gifts, and various other sacrifices of grandeur. Let not therefore this distress overwhelm you again on witnessing your friends, kin and relatives lying slain on the battlefield. You cannot see those men slain in this battle alive again. Therefore, you should perform grand sacrifices with gifts and donations, so that you would attain fame and renown in this world and reach the ultimate path.

11

Dhruva's Immortal Feat

This story from Shrimad Bhagavata Purana, is an interesting account of how a small child Dhruva achieved an immortal feat which no one ever achieved & received an astral place in the galaxies of universe.

In ancient times, Svayambhuva Manu had two descendants, his sons namely Uttanapada and Priyavrata. King Uttanapada had two wives, those queens were Suniti and Suruchi. The most favorite of the king was Suruchi, they had a son named Uttama. From Suniti, King had a son named Dhruva. There comes an incident on one day when Uttanapada while occupying on the royal throne in his court, called Uttama and placed him on his lap, however he did not give same treatment to Dhruva. Suruchi nastily took evil pleasure seeing the humiliation of prince Dhruva and uttered the vicious words to him as if some advice is given, "Dear Dhruva child," she said, "You are not worthy to sit on the king's lap because you have not taken birth from me. You are born from other woman and hence do not qualify for the same treatment. If you wish to have this throne as a seat you will have to carry out many tapas (severe austerities) and get blessings from the almighty lord with devotement and worship, by doing this, in your next birth, he will bestow you the privilege of getting born from me.

These tormenting words hurt a small prince of five years old, Dhruva. He rushed to his mother to recount the whole incident. Suniti was deeply hurt by the ill-treatment and injustice to her son, however she tried to calm her child, and taught Dhruva that he should never express any vicious words to anyone, because just like he felt hurt, others too will have to suffer the if the malice is inflicted on others. She said, "Although your stepmother Suruchi was harsh in her words, but she has a point. If you like to occupy the seat on your father's throne which the brother Uttama also enjoyed, you have to follow the path of meditation and start worshipping the almighty Lord. The Supreme Lord is so potent and kind that just by devotion at his lotus feet, your forebears were blessed. Your ancestor Brahma was bestowed with all powers required to bring the whole universe into being, and your grandfather Svayambhuva Manu achieved greater heights in both physical and spiritual worlds. You too should pursue the path of devotion and worship of the Lord, because only almighty can grant you what you desire."

Prince Dhruva seriously contemplated his mother's advice and right away left home to meditate and worship Lord Vishnu. Narada muni, the son of Brahma, become aware of what has happened and set off to search prince Dhruva. Stunned by his determination and strong will, he tried to convince the child that he is too young and go back to his home and mother. "You are of little age," he said, "At this age, you should enjoy playing and should not get bothered too much by someone's treatment. Moreover, due to the previous birth karmas the sufferings of living beings are caused. Your mother has suggested you follow the devotional path of the Lord through the means of mystic yoga, but it is a highly laborious task even for sanyasis, munis, and yogis, and many did not get success in achieving the goal after many birthtimes of practice."

However, Dhruva was so determined that he did not budge even little. He expressed sincere gratitude to Narada for his valuable advice and said he is unable to follow the advice because of his own weaknesses and considering the gravity of incident that just happened.

Narada was incredibly pleased with Dhruva's determination and developed empathy for this little child. Narada muni taught Dhruva how to worship Vishnu. Being grateful on his teaching, the little prince offered him deep respects and then travelled to the banks of river Yamuna, there in the forest called Madhuvana, he engaged in penances. Daily after taking three times bath, he sat on to deeply meditate on supreme lord, practiced breathing control or pranayama to rein in the Indriyas (senses) and mind.

As per Narada muni's advice, Dhruva also created an idol image of the lord using the river clay. By fixing his thoughts and concentration on the magnificent clay image of Lord Vishnu, daily he recited the mantra given by Narada with full devotion. As an offering to the Lord, he brought tulasi leaves, pure water, flowers, fruits, freshly sprouted grass found in the forest.

As little Dhruva was daily engrossed in strict austerities, worship, and meditational activities to transcend into his inner Self where Supreme Lord resides into every being,

Narada visited his father king Uttanapada. King Uttanapada was regretful about the ill treatment given to Dhruva and Suniti. He was deeply worried about his son, retired into the forest infested with full of dangers of wild animals and beasts. Narada Muni comforted the king by saying that Dhruva is not an ordinary person by any means, and that he would soon attain spiritual victory and return to his kingdom.

The strict regimen that Dhruva followed was that, in the first month he consumed only fruits and wild berries once every three days, during the second month he only ate grass and dry leaves once every six days and in the third month he drank just water every nine days without solid food, and in the fourth month he achieved complete control on breath and prana (life energy), with this perfection his body gained steadiness, senses controlled and the mind deeply absorbed into Supreme Soul of God residing in his own Self (Atman). Now having mastered his breath and completely stopped, Dhruva weighed so heavy that his body pressed the entire earth, the whole universe started shaking. All the celestial beings panicked with this situation, the Devas approached Lord Vishnu and prayed for his intervention. In order to allay the fear and panic of Devas, Lord Vishnu arrived in the forest of Madhuvana and brought out Dhruva from his intense austerity and meditation.

Seeing the Lord Vishnu himself appeared before him, Dhruva bowed down with profound respect, devotion and embraced the Lord. Dhruva offered delightful prayers to the Lord. Immensely pleased with Dhruva's devotion, Lord Vishnu blessed him by touching his forehead with

Moksha - The Immortal Bliss

his conchshell; the mere touch of this gave the little prince the perfect understanding of supreme goal of human soul, Vedic knowledge and blessings for all future paths and endeavors of Dhruva.

After gaining a rare wisdom which is hard to get by any living being, Dhruva realized how insignificant was his need for the search of God to attain place on the throne like his brother. He recognized that one who has attained the supreme Lord, all such desires of honor, status, material success and physical world and possessions become trivial and worthless. Dhruva found himself in a situation that when the bottomless ocean of treasure was opened for him by the Lord and what he had asked is just a handful of grains.

After bestowing the perfect spiritual wisdom and soul upliftment, with Vishnu's blessing, King Dhruva to rule on the entire world by as Uttanapada's heir for thousands of years in lasting youth. And as a destiny of their own karma, Uttama meets death while on the hunting expedition in the forest and his mother Suruchi lost her mental balance while looking for her son. Vishnu also rewarded Dhruva for the feat that no one ever achieved at such a tender age, Lord gave him the position of bright celestial body known as the Pole Star, that perpetually exist even though other planets have suffered destruction at the conclusion of Brahma's Day. Even today, Pole Star has a significant importance in the astronomical position. After leaving his physical body behind, Dhruva would still remember the realization of Supreme lord and attain the moksha & liberation from re-births.

After getting the news that Dhruva is returning home after achieving the perfect spiritual wisdom and Lord Vishnu's grace, Uttanapada travelled immediately to meet him with all his royal retinue. Immediately after seeing Dhruva, the king disembarked from his royal chariot and hugged him tightly, tears started flowing incessantly. Dhruva had been a transformed soul after he had gained the ultimate spiritual goal and realization. Not only his father and mother welcomed him with love but also Suruci and Uttama greeted Dhruva with warm heart. The whole kingdom of Uttanapada celebrated the return of young prince with festivals and decorations, they showered flowers and blessings on the procession of Dhruva.

After Uttanapada ruled the earth for many years happily with his family, he had retired into the forest for meditation and spiritual conquest during the last phase of his life before death. Dhruva was the installed on the royal throne and he ruled for many years. After completing his family and royal duties, Dhruva retired into the mountain of Himalayas in the forest of Badarikashrama & fully submerged himself on the Supreme Soul of God.

While leaving his physical mortal body behind, Dhruva were received by two graceful Vishnudutas known as Nanda and Sunanda on a divine space vehicle & carried his divine soul to spiritual world, Dhruvaloka.

12

Moksha of the Elephant Gajendra

This tale from Shrimad Bhagavata Purana, is an enchanting story of how elephant named Gajendra, on account of his perfect devotion and merits accrued from past life, reaches to the state of perfect liberation from endless cycles of birth and death.

The great Trikuta mountain standing majestically in the middle of milk-like ocean with its three principal peaks of iron, silver and gold shining incessantly. Other peaks in Trikuta mountain range were lush green with blooming trees, gigantic creepers and bushes, the scenic waterfalls and majestic caves were inhabited by celestial beings. Mountain valleys were adorned with heavenly gardens crowded by animals and cheerful birds. Amidst many rivers and lakes having beaches whose sands was like small pearls and precious gems. In a pure and crystal-clear water, beautiful and charming Apsaras come to bath leaving their perfumed body scent behind.

In one such garden named Ritumat, there were diverse species of trees & plants loaded with fruits and flowers. A great lake with innumerable lotus flowers blossoming with exquisite and rare plants relished by beetles and honeybees.

In Ritumat, a great and mighty king of elephants named Gajendra was living happily. On one sunny morning, while taking bath in a lake Gajendra was suddenly and viciously attacked by a crocodile. Even though having immense strength and power, the elephant was unable to free his leg from the clutches of crocodile. Gajendra tried so hard, but his leg was badly bitten, and all his struggles were going in vain for an exceedingly long time. As the time passed, Gajendra started losing out all his strength while monstrous size crocodile gained so much that it started pulling him into water with fierce hold.

Having finally understood that he has no chance to escape, Gajendra started exhorting God Vishnu, in a complete surrender to supreme lord and stopped fighting. Moving his trunk, he picked up a lotus flower from the lake and raised high as an offering it to the Lord together with devoutly prayer. Lord Vishnu seated on by Garuda, instantly appeared in front of Gajendra, and pulled both the elephant and the crocodile out of the water, then by his Sudarshana chakra he cut off the crocodile's head, thus rescuing his great devotee, Gajendra. Whole heaven and celestial beings danced and celebrated the rescuing of Gajendra and the emergence of the Lord, also for the crocodile who had returned to the original form as the king of Gandharvas. Gajendra was not only freed from his elephant's form but also attained the liberation called "Sarupya Mukti" taking a spiritual form like that of Lord Vishnu, in which he was attained immortal place in Vaikuntha.

Great devotee of Lord Vishnu from many births, in his previous lifetime, Gajendra had been a king named Maharaj Indradyumna in the Pandya province of south India. After ending his Gruhasthashram (Family Life), Indradyumna retired into Malaya hills & engaged in meditation on Vishnu. One day, when the king was observing silence vow, Agastya Muni appeared in his Ashram with his Shishyas (students). As the King could not welcome him due to the vow, as this conduct was against the Raja dharma or customs, the great Agastya Muni cursed him to take a new birth as an elephant.

This story of Gajendra Moksha is a perfect example of Bhakti Yoga. On the day of deliverance, the deep devotion, and prayers in any birth form, will not only rescue the devotee but has the power to bestow the supreme goal of life, liberation from endless cycle of births and deaths.

13

The Mahaprasthan - Yudhishthira's Ultimate Salvation

The concluding Mahaprasthanika parva of Mahabharata recounts the final journey of Pandavas & Draupadi and Yudhishthira reaching ultimate salvation which no other royal sage ever achieved.

A great battle ensued between Vrishni and the Andhaka races in which the Vrishnis (Yadava) perished, and Lord Krishna also departed to the heavenly abode of Vishnu. After hearing this news of decimation of Vrishnis, the King Yudhishthira started contemplating on leaving the world. He said to Arjuna, "O you of great wisdom, it is 'Time' that cooks every mortal being (in his big kettle). I believe whatever has taken place is due to the strings of Time (with which he straps us all). It befits you also to witness it."

Having heard these words from his brother, Arjuna uttered this word "Time, Time!" And then he had fully supported the view of his eldest brother endowed with great intellect. Confirming the decision of Arjuna, his brothers Bhimasena,

Nakula, and Sahdev fully backed the words that Arjuna had spoken.

Firmly determined to take retirement from the world for gaining virtue, they summoned Yuyutsu before their eyes. Yudhishthira gave him the responsibility of supervising the kingdom, Yuyutsu was the only survived son of his uncle Dhritarashtra born from Vaisya wife. By enthroning Parikshit, as a king, Yudhishthira addressed Arjuna's consort Subhadra with heavy heart, saying, this grandson of yours will now be the emperor of the Kurus. The last surviving inheritor of the Yadus, Vajra, will also be made as a king. Parikshit will reign in Hastinapura, whereas Vajra will govern Shakraprastha. They should be safeguarded by you. Never allow unrighteousness to overpower your mind.

After these conversations, Pandavas extended offerings of water to Vasudeva, Rama, also to his old maternal uncle and others. Yudhishthira then aptly performed the Sraddha rites (homage to ancestors) of all his departed kins and relatives. The great king of Hastinapur along with other Pandava brothers chanted the name of Hari and fed the Krishna Dvaipayana Vyasa, and Markandeya, Narada and Yajnavalkya of Bharadwajas, with many delicious food items. In the memory and respect of Krishna, he donated many jewels, gems, garments, and villages, and horses and carriages, and many material possessions to the best of Brahmanas. Sage Kripa is appointed as a royal preceptor and Parikshit was assigned as his disciple.

Then Yudhishthira convened all the citizens of kingdom, royal gurus notified them of Pandavas intentions. The citizens of the kingdom provinces became filled with unease and opposed of this decision. Please do not do this, they urged their king. Emperor Yudhishthira, well aware of the fate brought by the time could not agree with all whom tried to dissuade him and Pandavas.

With his virtuous soul, he convinced the people to approve his intentions and perspective. Determined to leave this world, Pandavas prepared themselves. Yudhishthira relinquished his royal jewelry and put on the barks of trees. Draupadi, Bhima, Arjuna and the twins also wore clothes made from bark.

After performing religious rites to get blessings, Pandavas released their sacred fires into the water. Citizens, royal ladies, and princes cried aloud and wept, in a comparable situation when in the past the Pandavas along with Draupadi left the Hastinapur for the forest exile after their defeat at the game of dice. But this time the Pandava brothers were very satisfied at the prospect of retirement. Confirming Yudhishthira's noble intentions and witnessing the decimation of the Vrishnis, no other action would have gratified them.

Five Pandavas, with Draupadi the sixth, and a dog the seventh, began their journey. All citizens, royal ladies, sages followed them till outskirts, but none of them could dare to say persuading words to Pandavas to give up their intentions, with heavy hearts they returned. Ulupi who is Arjuna's wife and the daughter of the Naga chief entered the waters of Ganga. The princess Chitrangada departed for the kingdom of Manipura. Yuyutsu and Parikshit stood supported by Kripa and remaining royal ladies.

Pandavas and Draupadi set out in the east direction. Placing themselves firmly on Yoga, and with vows of the religion of Renunciation, travelled through numerous regions and crossed many rivers and waters. Yudhishthira first in the order followed by Bhima and Arjuna; after them walked Nakula and Sahadeva in the order of the birth seniority and behind them Draupadi, the first royal woman. A dog too followed them keenly when they started out for the forest.

During this journey Arjuna had not left behind his great celestial bow Gandiva, and those inexhaustible quivers, due to the significant importance attached to it. Pandavas arrived at the sea of red waters. The Pandavas there witnessed the deity of fire stationed in front of them like a hill. That deity of seven flames talked to the Pandavas, 'Oh! brave heir of Pandu, I am the lord of fire. O Pandavas, hear out to what I say! You are the greatest of Kurus race, I am the god of fire. The Khandava forest was burned down by me, with the might of prince Arjuna and of Narayana (Krishna) himself. Let Arjuna continue to forest after forsaking Gandiva, that celestial weapon. This Gandiva was obtained by me from Varuna for Arjua, the Partha. Let it be offered to Varuna himself. He no longer needs any of this weapon. The divine discus (chakra) which was used by Lord Krishna has vanished (after his death) when again the opportune time arrives, it will be return into his hands.

After hearing what Agni said, all the Pandavas urged Arjuna to follow the instruction of the deity. Arjuna agreed and threw the Gandiva and inexhaustible quivers into the waters of Varuna, the lord of sea. Instantly, after this act of relinquishing weapon the fire deity disappeared. Pandavas then next continued towards the south direction. After crossing the northern shore of the salt sea, they progressed to the south-west. Going by the west direction, they reached near to the city of Dwaraka submerged by the ocean. Then they moved further to the north. Resolutely fixed on Yoga, they aspired of having a trip round of the whole Earth.

In the north, they reached Himavat, a large mountain range. After surpassing the Himavat, they arrived at a vast sand desert. Here they saw the majestic mountain Meru, the supreme amongst tallest mountains. As these brothers were moving quickly, engrossed in Yoga (ascetic journey), Yajnaseni Draupadi, fell down on the ground. Holding her mortal body, powerful Bhimasena asked king Yudhishthira, O great conqueror of enemies, this princess had never committed any sinful and yet, what the reason that she has fallen on the earth!

Yudhishthira said, "O Bhimasena, for her, we all brothers were all equal, but she had a bias towards Dhananjaya (Arjuna). She has reaped the fruit of her doings today, O foremost of men."

Pandavas proceeded further on their journey. After a while, Sahadeva of spiritual knowledge and wisdom dropped down on the earth. Seeing him falling down, Bhima asked the king, "He had served all of us with great humility, still, why is this son of Madravati falling down on the earth?"

Yudhishthira said, "Sahadeva never thought anybody is his equal in knowledge and wisdom. It is for this weakness that this prince has met with this fate and fallen down."

The king and Pandavas proceeded further leaving Sahadeva there. Yudhishthira with other brothers and the dog continued their journey. Having witnessed Draupadi and the Sahadeva fallen down, the spirited Nakula who always greatly loved family and kins, fell down himself. After heroic Nakula, with great physical beauty met his fate, Bhima again asked the king, "This brother of ours who embodied perfect righteousness, always obeyed his elders, and bestowed with unmatched beauty, has fallen down."

Having mentioned this by Bhima, Yudhishthira replied, after paying respect to Nakula, he said, "He was virtuous soul and blessed with intelligence. He, however, assumed that nobody has equaled him in personal beauty and considered himself as a superior in this physical attribute. It is because of this reason that Nakula has gone down. Learn this, O Vrikodara (Bhima), person has to endure, what is laid down for him."

Falling down of Nakula, Sahadeva and Draupadi were watched by Arjuna, the great slayer of enemies, he fell down with an enormous grief in the heart. When Arjuna, the bravest of men, possessed with Indra's energy had fallen down Bhima address the King Yudhishthira, "I do not remember Arjuna ever uttered any untruth and not even in quip, then why did this evil befallen on him?"

Yudhishthira answered, "Arjuna said he will vanquish all our enemies in a single day. Proudly boasted his bravery, he could not do that; however, he still accomplished the extermination of enemies. Therefore, Arjuna has fallen down. Arjuna ignored all wielders of bow with a slight. Such a tendency should not be kept by someone having high-soul aspirations."

Having spoken so, the king went on further in his path. The Bhima following him from behind dropped down. That time, Bhimsena addressed king Yudhishthira, saying, "O king, look, I who is your dearest have fallen down. For what caused my descending down? Kindly tell me if you know it."

Yudhishthira said, "You had been a great devourer, and you boasted your strength. You never paid attention what others wanted while eating food. This is the reason of that, O Bhima, you have fallen."

Having said these words, the Son of Dharma Yudhishthira continued his ascent, without turning back. He had only one companion now, the dog which had never stopped following him.

The King of Gods, Indra, arrived with loud thunder reverberating in the firmament and the earth. Indra riding on carriage came near to the son of Pritha (Kunti), Yudhishthira and asked him to ascend it. Staring at his brothers dropped on the earth, king Yudhishthira told to that god of a thousand eyes, "My brothers have all dropped down here. They must accompany with me. I have no intention of going to heaven without them, O ruler of all Devas. The exquisite princess Draupadi worthy of all happiness, O Purandara, she should come with us. By permitting this, such treatment will be befitting to you."

Indra answered, "You shall have your brothers in heaven. They have reached heaven before you. In fact, you will see them there, with Draupadi. O Yudhishthira do not give up in the grief. After leaving their mortals, they have reached there. And for you, it is decreed that you shall attain heaven in this very physical body of yours."

Yudhishthira said, "O lord of the three dimensions of time, this dog, he is exceptionally faithful and dedicated to me. He must come with me. My heart is filled with compassion for him."

Indra replied, "You have won the Immortality and status equivalent to mine, where prosperity, success and blissfulness are rolling in all directions. If you leave this dog here, it is not going to be cruelty."

Yudhishthira replied, "O lord with thousand eyes. O you are of virtuous behaviour, it is extremely tough for someone that is virtuous to commit an act which is non-virtuous. I do not want to join such bliss for which I will have to abandon the one who is devoted and faithful to me."

Indra replied, "There is no berth in heaven for persons having dogs. Furthermore, Krodhavasas deities strip down all the virtuous credits of such persons. Considering this, O king Yudhishthira, leave this dog. It is not cruelty to do so."

Yudhishthira replied, "It has been mentioned that the deserting one who is dedicated is immensely sinful and equivalent to the sin that one accrues by killing a Brahmana. Therefore, O eminent Indra, I would not leave this dog behind driven by my desire of happiness. Nevertheless, it is my pledge which I had constantly adhered, that by no means, I abandon a person that is frightened, which is devoted to me and sought my protection, the one who he is poor and in trouble coming to me, one who is weak in defending oneself and worried for his life. I shall not once abandon such a one until my very own life is at end."

Indra said, "All the sacrifices, gifts and offerings tendered to the sacred fire if seen by a dog are snatched away by Krodhavasas. For this reason, you should give up this dog. By leaving this dog behind, you will attend the realm of devas. With your brothers and Draupadi abandoned, you alone have achieved a blissful region. What is the reason of your confusion? You have renounced everything, why are you not renouncing this dog?"

Yudhishthira said, "It is very well-known fact that those who are departed from this world, they are neither friend nor enemy of anyone. When my brother and Draupadi passed away, I was not able to revive them, hence I had to leave them behind. Till they were alive, I never left them. To terrify someone, who has secured your protection, killing a woman, stealing from the custody of Brahmana, and harming a friend, each one of these four, O Indra, I think is same as leaving off someone which is devoted and faithful to you."

Having heard the speech of king Yudhishthira, the dog got transformed into Dharma, the deity of just and righteousness, who, extremely pleased, said following words in full of praise of king, in a cheerful voice.

Dharma said, "You are truly having good breeding, O king of Kings, having intelligence and gentility of Pandu. You are full of compassion for all beings, O Bharata, this one is such a shining example. In the past, O son, you were judged by me in the forest of Dwaita, where your brothers suffered death, by setting aside your own brothers you wished for the revival of Nakula, for doing good to your deceased stepmother. In this present situation, showing compassion to the dog devoted to you, you were ready to abandon the vehicle to the celestial instead of abandoning him. That is why, O king, not a single soul is there in heaven which is equal to you. O Bharata, the region of blissfulness is for you. You have deserved it, yours is divine and supreme goal."

Then all the Deities, joined by Dharma, Indra, the Ashvins and the Maruts and the divine Rishis, prompting Yudhishthira to mount on a carriage, carried on to heaven. Those deities who were accomplished and adept of venturing anywhere at will, mounted on their personal cars. King Yudhishthira, that greatest amongst Kurus race, rode on to that celestial vehicle, causing the whole sky to illuminate with brightness. Then Narada, that supreme amongst all speakers, with great ascetic powers, and abreast with whole universe and worlds, in the middle of assembly of deities, said, "Yudhishthira has surpassed all those royal sages who attained heaven. Encompassing all the worlds by his immortality and brilliance, and on account of his exemplary conduct, he has earned heaven in his mortal (human) body. None other than this scion of Pandu has been ever witnessed to accomplish this feat."

14

Bhrigu's Immortal Bliss

This mystical tale is from Taittiriya Upanishad's third chapter Bhrigu Valli. In Sanskrit, the word Valli means a creeper, like a creeper grows vertically if a standing support is provided similarly the valli represents one's growth or maturity, mainly the spiritual growth which is always upwards. Upanishads seeks the meaning of "Brahman" the supreme soul which is a source of every creation and resides in every being. Such is a tale of one such seeker, Bhrigu.

One day Bhrigu, the son of Varuna, came to his father Varuna and requested, "Honorable Sir, I want to know Brahman, teach me." Varuna replied, "Food, the essential breath, the eye, the ear, the mind, speech." Varuna implied here by saying that these all are orginated from Brahman and they together should be pursued to know what Brahmana is.

To Bhrigu his father further replied, "The one from which living beings are born, the one by which, once born, they live, the one into which these beings get into, and they unite—pursue that one to know. That one is Brahman. Seek the knowledge of Brahman using austerities. Austerities are the way to know Brahman."

So, Bhrigu performed severe austerities and penance.

Bhrigu learnt that- "Food is Brahman; truly from food the living beings are born; after they are born these living beings subsist on food, and when born, they live, they enter, and they merge into food."

But with this, Bhrigu's quest was not satiated because even food has beginning and end.

So, he approached his father again and said: "Respected Sir, teach me Brahman." over this, Varuna replied: "Seek the knowledge of Brahman using austerities. Austerities are the way to know Brahman." He conducted austerities. After going through austerities:

Bhrigu learnt that- "Breath is Brahman; truly from breath these living beings are born; when born these living beings live by breath, and when born, they live, they enter, they merge into breath."

But again, Bhrigu sensed that breath is not having intelligence of its own.

So, he went to his father again and said: "Respected Sir, teach me Brahman." over this, Varuna replied: "Seek the knowledge of Brahman using austerities. Austerities are the way to know Brahman." He conducted austerities. After going through austerities:

Bhrigu learnt that- "Mind is Brahman; truly from mind the living beings are born; when born these living beings live by breath, and when born, they live, they enter, and they merge into mind."

This time a doubt came to Bhrigu's mind, since the mind is another sensory organ and it gives rise to emotions and desires, how can it be Brahman.

So, he went to his father again and said, "Respected Sir, teach me Brahman." over this, Varuna replied, "Seek the knowledge of Brahman using austerities. Austerities are the way to know Brahman."

He conducted austerities. After going through austerities, Bhrigu learnt that- "Intellect is Brahman; truly from intellect these beings are born; when born these living beings live by intellect, and when born, they live, they enter, and they merge into intellect."

Now he learns that intellect is a driver of the mind in a specific path. And Intellect gives ability to discriminate between what is right and wrong. So, intellect could be Brahman but, the different responses to sensations are determined by Intellect and hence intellect cannot be that one whom he is seeking.

So, he went to his father again and said, "Respected Sir, teach me Brahman." over this, Varuna replied: "Seek the knowledge of Brahman using austerities. Austerities are the way to know Brahman." He conducted austerities. After going through austerities:

He finally gets enlightenment that "Bliss is Brahman" (Param Ananda is Para Brahma) and truly from Bliss (Param Ananda), are all living beings are born; when born they live by bliss, and when born, they live into bliss, at the ultimate time of conclusion, they enter, and they merge into bliss.

This is the profound wisdom taught by Varuna and self-realized by Bhrigu. It is placed in the superior vault, in the heart. He who has this knowledge and realized his presence, is engrossed in the Bliss of Brahman.

This story in short, tells us that with step-by-step course of austerities and meditation on Brahman reaching finally to moksha. First by understanding and then peeling each of those sheaths namely food or matter *(annamaya kosha)*, breath *(pranamaya kosha)*, mind *(manomaya kosha)* and intellect *(vijnanamaya kosha)*, the true seeker can attain to layer of immortal bliss *(ananda maya kosha)*, in which that Supreme Soul or Brahman dwells.

15

Mudgala's Emancipation & Immortal Bliss

Once upon a time, in the region of Kurukshetra lived a righteous man, by name Mudgala. He was truthful, pure minded and having controlled senses. He lived his life by collecting left aways from the corn field, like ears of corn and small piece of grains, what remains after farmers have cut and taken away the sheaves; this Satvik (pure) mode of life followed by him, and his family is based on gathering the left-over grains.

Even though having livelihood like a pigeon, still this one of the greatest ascetics hosted his guests and performed the sacrifice named Istikrita & devotedly carried out this and other rites. Mudgala along with his son and wife used to eat only during one fortnight and while in other fortnight lived like a pigeon collecting left aways in one drona of grain of corn. He observed to new moon and full moon sacrificial rites and the honest him, ate only whatever remains after offering to deities and guests. On bright lunar days, the lord of heavens himself in company with other deities would come to partake their share of the offering. Mudgala, living life a like a sage, with a joyful heart treated his guests with food. When this big hearted one served his food with cheery spirit, whatever remained in drona increased whenever the guest come to visit. By the power of his pure soul giving away, the food increased with so much quantity that hundreds of learned brahmans were served by him. After getting to know about the noble Mudgala of high qualities, Rishi Durvasa barely cladded in anything, dressed like that of lunatic and shaven head came to him and spoke insultingly unpleasant words. Having arrived, that supreme of all Munis Rishi Durvasa spoke to Mudgala, 'O you best of brahmana, I have come here desiring for food.' Mudgala replied, 'You are welcome!' He first offered that hungry lunatic of an ascetic, water to cleanse his feet and mouth, then with deep respect served excellent food which he had earned with great ordeals. The starving Muni Durvasa ate up all the food offered to him, then Mudgala again served him with more food. After eating up everything offered to him, Durvasa stained his body with leftover food & left the way he had arrived. As there was no food left over by Durvasa, drona of corn did not get replenished. In similar way, again on a bright lunar day, Muni Durvasa came again and consumed all the food served by the one who lived on collecting the leftover grain of corns from field. Furthermore, without eating any food himself, the sage Mudgala had to again go to collect corn. But Mudgala's hunger failed to trouble his composure. No infliction of anger, humiliation, unrest, came to the minds of that foremost of brahmana, his son and wife. In such a manner, Muni Durvasa with the strong determination arrived for six successive times before the Mudgala who lived on collected grains. But Muni could not find any turbulence in Mudgala's mind, and he discovered that his mind is as pure as his soul and always refined. Extremely pleased Muni Durvasa spoke to Mudgala, 'On this earth, there is no other pure and beneficent being like you. The pain of hunger drives out the ethical sense of righteousness and tolerance. The tongue relishes on tasty food and attaches the men to senses. Life is supported by the food. Mind is volatile and hard to keep in control. Directing the mind and senses is a hallmark of asceticism. It is tough to give up with a pure mind the things which are earned with toil and pain. However, O holy one, all this has been accomplished by you. We feel indebted and gladdened to have met you. Self-control, Controlling the senses, endurance, hospitality, reigning the senses, composure, compassion, and righteousness are all residing in you. By your deeds, you have won the worlds & achieved the entry into path of bliss. Ah! In fact, the residents of heaven are declaring your remarkable deeds of charity. O you committed to vows! you shall attain heaven in your physical body. At the same when Muni Durvasa had this conversation, angelic messenger of the gods shown up before Mudgala, in a heavenly chariot yoked to swans and cranes and had string of bells. Chariot was divinely scented, beautifully painted and could travel anywhere it wish to. Messenger spoke to Mudgala, 'O Sage, mount the chariot. You have earned it by your deeds. You have achieved the fruits of your austerities!' as the emissary of gods was conversing thus, the sage Mudgala told him, "O celestial messenger, I would like that you may narrate me the traits of the resident of heaven. What are their sacrifices and their determinations? And what consist of the celestial joy in heaven and what are the drawbacks of it?

Wise men of noble lineage have proclaimed that seven paces together are what all that is needed for a friendship with virtuous. O exalted one! through that friendship, I beg you, 'Unhesitatingly, tell me the truth and what is set down for me. After hearing you, I will decide my course according to your words.'"

That emissary of the gods said, "O eminent sage, you have secured that divine bliss which bestows great honour, are you still deliberating like the person who is not wise? O sage, know that this region of heaven exists above us. Those higher up regions have magnificent streets and busy with the celestial carriages of gods. O sage, men who have not subjected themselves with stern austerities, those who have not performed noble sacrifices, deceitful and atheists cannot reach there. Only men of souls with virtuousness and subjugated their souls, those who have senses controlled, those who do bear envy, persons devoted to charity and brave ones bearing scars from battle, attain it. With restrained senses and wits, having practiced most deserving sacrificial rites, O brahmana, those worlds can be obtained only by righteous acts and populated by virtuous men. O Mudgala! There exists plenty of pretty, glowing, and brilliant independent worlds conferring each and every object of wish, ruled by divine beings, the gods, the sadhyas, the vishwadevas, the maha-rishis, the yamas, the dhamas, the gandharvas and the apsaras. The emperor amongst all mountains, the golden Meru spanning over a thirty-three thousand yojanas is there. O Mudagala, the blissful gardens are there with Nandana Garden the main one where persons with worthy deeds can enjoy.

There is no hunger, thirst, fatigue, fear, or anything that is hateful or evil. That place is filled with aromas which are pleasant, and breezes are charming to touch. The sounds are enchanting to the ear and the heart. There is no sorrow, feebleness, no pain, no remorse. O sage, that world is attained as a result of one's own deeds. Person gets rejuvenated on account of their excellent deeds. Inhabitants of that world look splendid and O Mudagala, this is purely on account of their self-acts, not due to merits of their parents. You will not find there the sweat, stink, or urine. And O sage, dust do not smear clothes. Their exquisite garlands, scented of celestial fragrance, never wane. And O brahmana, they harness such vehicles (that I am riding). Those regions completely lack jealousy, sorrow, lethargy, ignorance and ill will and persons who have obtained heaven, reside in those worlds merrily. And O great among sages, as we advance further in higher realms over these regions, these are inhabited by those filled with greater spiritual virtues. Out of these, Brahma's dazzling and splendid regions are the supreme. Towards that side, O brahmana, Rishis who have purified themselves with virtuous deeds are departed. In that world, beings called as Ribhus reside, who are deities of gods itself. Regions of Ribhus are exceedingly beatified and revered even by deities. These regions illuminate by its own shine and confer each and every thing of desire. Ribhus are not distressed by the infliction, they have no material riches, they are free from cunningness. They are neither dependent on sacrificial oblations (offerings) nor on amrita (ambrosia). They are empowered with such a divine form that they cannot be seen by our senses. These immortal gods of heavens neither lust after happiness nor do they get transformed at the end of Kalpa (or many thousand years). Then where is their infirmity or end? for Ribhus there is no euphoria, no rejoice, no pleasure. When they do not have happiness or sorrow, how they will have anger or dislike? O Mudgala, their highest state is even desired by the gods. That ultimate emancipation which is difficult to obtain can never be achieved by person keeping desires. Those are thirty-three deities. Those men of wisdom reach these worlds, after adhering to admirable vows of austerity or donate gifts in charity according to rites.

You have also comfortably secured that achievement by the virtue of your charities. Radiant splendor generated by your ascetic practices, deserves that state on account of your virtuous deeds. O brahmana, such is a blissfulness of the world of heaven consists of different regions.

Having described you the favours of the heavenly regions, listen now from me some of the defects of it. That in the heaven, a person while acquiring the fruits of his deeds carried out, he cannot be occupied in other acts, and he should relish on the after-effects of the previous deeds till those are fully consumed. After he has completely spent his accrued merits, he is subjected to fall, this is in my view the pitfall of heaven. The descend of a man whose conscious is saturated in a bliss must be proclaimed as a pitfall. The dissatisfaction and remorse that follows after one has relished more favorable and bright regions must be unbearable. Stirred by emotions, the consciousness of descending person becomes numb and overpowered by fear, as the garlands wore by them is decayed. O Mudgala, these big flaws are stretched even to the higher worlds of Brahma. In the heavenly worlds, there are innumerable merits of the men engaged in virtuous acts. On account of these virtuous deeds, they take birth on the earth & achieves greater luck and happiness. But after taking birth, if one does not acquire wisdom here, they happen to get inferior birth. The consequence of the deeds done in this world are earned in the next birth. Thus, this world, O brahmana has been proclaimed as that of actions and other as that of the consequence of those actions or fruit. O Mudgala, as enquired by you, thus I have described you all. O virtuous one, with your acceptance, we shall smoothly depart with pace.

Upon hearing this address, Mudgala started thinking. And having pondered thoroughly, the best of sage spoke to god's emissary, "O messenger of the gods, I pay you my sincere obeisance. Take a leave in peace. I have no connection either with joy or heaven having such major flaws. Men who revel in heaven endure suffering and great anguish in this world. Hence, I do not wish heaven. I will pursue departing for that eternal region where no one has to weep, suffer, or distressed. You have explained me these major flaws related to heavenly worlds. Please describe me a region free from flaws."

On that the god's messenger replied, 'Higher above the quarters of Brahma, there is a highest place of Shri Vishnu, the flawless, eternal, and radiant known as Para Brahma. O brahmana, in that region those persons cannot depart who have materialistic attachment of senses, nor those who are vulnerable to egotism, greed, lacks knowledge, anger and jealous. That region is only for those that are unconfined from the desire, pride, and inharmonious emotions, and those who have controlled the senses, devoted to meditation and yoga can rehabilitate there. After listening to these words, sage Mudgala bade adieu to the god's messenger, and that with an excellent virtue living the life on left aways, achieved perfect fulfillment. And then honour and dishonour turned equal to him, and a brick, rock and precious metals received the same treatment in his eyes. Devoted towards attaining Para Brahma (Supreme Soul), he immersed himself in the meditation. Mudgala attained that highest state of emancipation, which is regarded as "Immortal Bliss," by the virtue of knowledge and excellent wisdom.

Bibliography

Ganguli, Kisari Mohan. The Complete Mahabharata in English: The Mahabharata of Krishna-Dwaipayana Vyasa. Translated into English Prose from the Original Sanskrit Text, [1883-1896].

Shastri, Hari Prasad. The Ramayana of Valmiki: A Complete Modern English Translation, All 3 volumes combined, Burleigh Press, Great Britain, 1952.

Dutt, Manmatha Nath. The Ramayana, Translated into English Prose from the original Sanskrit of Valmiki, Volume 1 Balakandam, Edited and Published, Printed by Girish Chandra Chackravarti, Deva Press, Kolkata (Calcutta). 1891.

Sethumadhavan T. N. Taittiriya Upanishad, Transliterated Sanskrit Text, Free Translation & Brief Explanation. Published In esamskriti.com, 27th October 2011.

Swami Paramananda, The Upanishads, Translated and Commented, From the original Sanskrit Text, Volume 1, Third Edition, Published by Vedanta Center, Boston, MA, 1919.

Devi Parama Karuna Bhagavata Purana abridged translation by published by Jagannatha Vallabha Vedic Research Center 2016.

Debroy Bibek. Mahabharata, The: Volume 2 and Volume 3 paperback, Published by Penguin Books Ltd, 2015.

Joshi K. L., Bimali O.N. Trivedi Bindiya. 112 Upanishads Published by Parimal Publications, fifth edition, 2016.

www.ingramcontent.com/pod-product-compliance
Lightning Source LLC
LaVergne TN
LVHW061551070526
838199LV00077B/6994